The
Keys to
Kindness

Also by Claudia Hammond

Emotional Rollercoaster: A Journey Through the Science
of Feelings
Time Warped: Unlocking the Mysteries of Time
Perception
Mind Over Money: The Psychology of Money and How
to Use it Better
The Art of Rest: How to Find Respite in the Modern Age

The
Keys to
Kindness

How to Be Kinder to Yourself, Others and the World

Claudia Hammond

CANONGATE

First published in Great Britain, the USA and Canada in 2022
by Canongate Books Ltd, 14 High Street, Edinburgh EH1 1TE

Distributed in the USA by Publishers Group West
and in Canada by Publishers Group Canada

canongate.co.uk

1

British Library Cataloguing-in-Publication Data
A catalogue record for this book is available on
request from the British Library

ISBN 978 1 83885 444 7
Export ISBN 978 1 83885 445 4

Typeset in Garamond MT Std 11.5/15 pt by
Palimpsest Book Production Ltd, Falkirk, Stirlingshire

Printed and bound in Great Britain by Clays Ltd, Elcograf S.p.A.

To Fiona, who is always kind

CONTENTS

INTRODUCTION

I used to live not far from Abbey Road in London. When occasionally I drove along it, I was always super alert as I approached a certain zebra crossing. This crossing was immediately outside the famous Abbey Road Studios where the Beatles recorded most of their iconic albums, including of course, in 1969, *Abbey Road*. The reason for my caution was that there was invariably a group of tourists on the crossing – one of them barefooted, none of them paying heed to the traffic – who were intent on reproducing the shot of John, Ringo, Paul and George from the album cover, while a friend or passer-by took a photo of their homage to the Fab Four.

The Beatles are of course among the most famous people who have ever lived – feted and adored by millions. But the grand monument, in the middle of a junction close to the zebra crossing, has not been erected to honour their achievements. This monument is perhaps 18 feet tall and built of grey stone. On one of its plinths, there is a bronze sculpture of a muse playing the harp. On the other, there is a copper roundel depicting a distinguished, bearded face of a man in noble profile. Two grand lamp standards stand guard on either side of the monument. Who could warrant such a lavish memorial? And why was it erected?

The monument is to a Victorian sculptor called Edward Onslow Ford. So that's the who part. But I've always found the why part particularly heartwarming. Because the reason Onslow Ford's memory was marked in so striking a way was that he was so popular with his students and other sculptors for his 'charming disposition' that they raised a considerable sum to build this large memorial to him after his death in 1901. Letters of condolence to his widow in his archive housed at the Henry Moore Foundation speak of his great kindness. The inscription on the memorial reads: 'Erected by his friends and admirers. To thine own self be true.'

There are, I think, important lessons from the story of Onslow Ford, who it seems did succeed in being true to himself. First, it shows that we do value kindness to some extent – enough in exceptional cases to erect monuments to people who personify it. But second, it shows we perhaps don't value it enough. Compared with the Beatles, Onslow Ford's lasting impact on our culture is fairly minimal, so despite his memorial, my guess is that soon he will be pretty much forgotten, while the Beatles will surely be remembered for decades (even centuries?) to come. Genius and achievement are rightly revered. I'm not for a moment suggesting we should devalue these attributes. But I am suggesting that we should, like Onslow Ford's friends, notice and treasure the humbler virtue of kindness more than we sometimes do.

To this end, *The Keys to Kindness* makes the argument for taking kindness more seriously and valuing it more deeply. We are kinder than we might think, but we could be kinder still – with enormous benefits for our personal mental health and well-being, as well as for society, the economy and the environment. Using the latest psychological evidence from around the world, and drawing on a new and unique study, I will demonstrate that kindness helps not just others, but us too.

Being kind is not always easy though. The way the world is currently constructed can lead us to be tough on ourselves and on others. Schools, universities and workplaces are in some ways kinder places than they once were. Gone are the days when it was OK to throw a typewriter at someone (when I was new to a radio newsroom, older colleagues would tell me tales of such events). Gone are the days when children were caned for failing to remember their times tables. But across society, a premium is still put on personal achievement and individual success, often at the expense of others and sometimes through developing a hard and ruthless streak in ourselves. The idea can still get into us that to be kind is to be weak and that weakness means you lose out. I will be challenging that notion, backed up by extensive evidence that we all benefit from greater cooperation and compassion, and that being kind and empathic certainly isn't an impediment to success or even acclaim. More than that, the more kindness there is, the more the world will benefit.

I will also look into the tricky question of how to define what kindness is.

For instance, I wonder how many of these statements relate to you?

- I think it's right to give everyone a chance
- I find it easy to forgive
- I share things I would rather keep for myself
- I have surprised another person with an act of kindness
- I smile at strangers
- I've done something that upset me to help a friend

Don't worry if you don't identify with all of these statements. They represent some of the different types of kindness, so you may be more inclined towards tolerance or empathy, but less inclined towards taking deliberate actions to be kind or avoiding acts which might be unkind. Most likely, you have acted in all these ways on some occasions, but not on others. You are probably a kind person, but not all the time and you show your kindness in different ways at different times.

Kindness, you see, is not simple. Nor is it just one thing. It is multifaceted, hard to pin down and often misunderstood. I once offended the widower of a brilliant researcher by telling him that despite only having met his wife on a few short occasions I could tell what a really kind person she was. I meant it as a true compliment, but he felt the praise was rather bland and patronising, downplaying his wife's professional achievements. His reaction was perhaps understandable, particularly given the routine devaluation of women's accomplishments in traditionally male arenas. But even so, it was a shame – an instance of the attribute of kindness being under-appreciated in our culture. I'd like to live in a world where the greatest thing you could say about a person is that they were kind.

Seven Keys to Kindness

In this book, I explore seven keys to kindness, some of which may seem obvious to you, others less so. No one key is more important than any other; instead they fit together to provide a full picture of all aspects of kindness which we need to consider in order to make the world a kinder place.

In Chapter 1, I start by exploring the fact – often under-appreciated – that there is a lot of kindness in the world already. Yes, that's right. Humanity outweighs inhumanity – we just need to open our eyes to it and not be misled by the negativity that inevitably predominates in the news and on social media. Then in Chapter 2 I'll be showing that kindness is good for you, the giver, as well as for your beneficiaries. In fact, it's a win/win/win – for us as individuals, for others and for the wider world. In this chapter and the next, I'll show that people who act in kind ways benefit from their kindness – and I hope to convince you there is nothing wrong with that and that the advantages that accrue to you don't undermine the impact of your kindness on others. Then, I'll swerve slightly to discuss one of the big issues of our times: social media. In a 'half-chapter' entitled: 'Social media is full of kindness (OK, not full, but it is there)', I'll argue that while Twitter and Facebook and other platforms can be full of abuse and hatred, that is only half the story – even in these bear pits, kindness and positivity still flourish. In the next full chapter, I'll turn to a deeper exploration of the issue of whether you can be kind *and* be a winner in life. I hope this isn't a spoiler if I tell you now that the answer is a clear YES. I'll show that kindness is not soft, it's not weak; indeed, it can be our hidden strength.

Then comes the difficult question of how to be kinder. The fifth key to kindness is to take the trouble to understand other people's opinions and perspectives if we are to act kindly, but also that we should choose our moment. There is a time and a place for empathy. In the sixth chapter, I will argue that we don't have to confine ourselves to those small random acts of kindness that we hear so much about. We can think big. Most of us will never need to show huge bravery, but we're all capable of heroism and we can plan in advance for what might be a once in a lifetime opportunity to save a life. Also, thinking about extreme kindness can help us to be kinder in everyday life. Chapter 7 is a bit different because it doesn't concern kindness to others, but to ourselves. Self-care and self-compassion, I'll argue, need not slip into self-indulgence and selfishness, and done in the right way can have huge benefits for our mental health. We need to develop a true tenderness towards ourselves and our failings, so that we can protect our well-being, and that puts us in a better position to help others.

I wrap things up with a prescription for kindness, with tips on how to put all this research into practice in order to be a kinder person and to build a kinder world. Here you can choose which suggestions might work in your life and I hope it will prompt you into thinking up your own ideas for acting in a more kindly way.

Throughout this book I will draw on hard evidence and proven strategies published in scientific journals. During the last two decades a topic which had been neglected within psychology and neuroscience has been studied in depth by experienced scientists. I stress this because it would be easy to dismiss a book about kindness as slushy, sentimental and lacking in rigour. The opposite is true.

The Kindness Test

I will also be making extensive use of brand new findings from the world's largest study of its type into kindness – the Kindness Test, on which I worked with colleagues at the

University of Sussex, a leading centre for kindness research. The research was led by Professor Robin Banerjee, sometimes nicknamed (by me anyway) 'the professor of kindness'. I launched the study on the BBC shows and podcasts I present – *All in the Mind* on BBC Radio 4 and *Health Check* on the BBC World Service.

In the Kindness Test we invited people to complete a series of online questionnaires, asking questions on everything from their personality and their mental health, to how kind they are in everyday life and what proportion of an unexpected cash windfall they might be prepared to give away. We were staggered by the number of people who chose to take part – 60,227 people from 144 countries. The analysis of this unprecedented data set gives us a richer understanding of how kindness really works in real life, and what it is that prevents from us from being kinder.

At the outset, the Kindness Test illustrated neatly how many types of kindness exist. When asked to list the ways in which they were kind, participants gave a huge number of examples, but here are the top five:

TOP FIVE WAYS PEOPLE TOLD US THEY WERE KIND

1. I help people when they ask
2. I don't mind doing favours for friends
3. I open doors to let people through
4. I help strangers pick up things they have dropped
5. I have concerned feelings for people less fortunate than me

---

What is striking is how everyday, even mundane, these actions are. They aren't huge acts of generosity or self-sacrifice. In fact, 'I don't mind doing favours for friends' might even sound a little grudging. But these small instances of kindness are happening all around us, often unnoticed, all the time. They may be small drops, but together they make an ocean. Given this, it is perhaps not surprising – though still heartening – that the study showed that kindness is very common and widespread. Three quarters of people said they received kindness from close friends or family 'quite often' or 'nearly all the time'. Fifty-nine per cent had received an act of kindness within the last day, and a quarter of those said it was in the last hour.

In the questionnaire, we also asked people to fill in a scale which rated their levels of kindness. Now, of course, we had to trust people to be honest about the kind acts they carry out, but the range of responses we received suggests that people are prepared to admit to *not* being especially kind as well as the opposite, so I think we can take people at their word and regard the scoring system as pretty robust.

The findings are interesting, particularly when it comes to categorising people who gained higher than average kindness scores. First, women and religious people report carrying out slightly more kind acts than average. But personality made much more of a difference. People who are extraverted, open to new experiences and agreeable, both give and, strikingly, receive more kindness. Value systems are also an important factor, more important than religion. Those who say they value benevolence and universalism are kinder on average than those who value achievement and power. But fear not if you are an ambitious, reserved, irritable, agnostic man. This doesn't mean you would automatically score low on kindness. These findings reflect what happens on average within a large group, so it's perfectly possible for a grumpy, introverted man, who strives for success and doesn't believe in God to still score very high on kindness. (Maybe you know a few?) However, the average scores still tell us something significant about who at the group level is most likely to be kind.

Another thing we asked in the Kindness Test was for people to list the words they associated with kindness. The top five in this case were:

TOP FIVE WORDS PEOPLE ASSOCIATED WITH KINDNESS

1. Empathy
2. Care
3. Helping
4. Thoughtfulness
5. Compassion

These are not, of course, particularly unexpected words and indeed they pretty much match how researchers in the field have conceptualised kindness. Within academia, however, there is considerable debate over precise terms and definitions. Yes, even people studying kindness find plenty to argue about, especially if talking about what constitutes *pure* kindness.

The Kindness Test is again helpful here, because it allows me to take a 'trust the people' approach. Of course, there's considerable, even great, kindness in steeling yourself to tell somebody something that's hard to hear, but which will help them in the long run. Of course, some kindness involves self-sacrifice, even pain. And then there are cases of long-considered altruism such as the donation of a kidney to a stranger. Or there are the spur of the moment heroic acts where a huge personal risk is taken and a life is saved. But at the same time, the everyday acts recorded in the test – the many thousands of cups of tea made, the hot baths run, the compliments given, the thank you cards sent, the smiles in shops, the dropped tickets handed back to their owners – are commonly understood as kindness and should be appreciated as such.

And in practice, there is a lot of overlap between the various types of kindness. A kind act can include heroism or gratitude or sympathy or love or care or compassion – or a combination of any of these. Being kind to strangers, regardless of the circumstances, is self-sacrificing in one sense, yet it brings pleasure to a person who acts in this way. Kindness might involve taking opportunities to be kind only when they present themselves, or actively seeking out every opportunity to act in kindly ways towards others – through volunteering, for example. Sometimes kindness involves seeing another person's perspective and viewing all their actions with compassion, but it might also involve intervening to tell a person that they are acting with disregard for others. Sometimes you have to be cruel to be kind, but of course you can be kind in gentler ways too. And while it might seem you can never be too kind, there is truth in the old saying that you can kill with kindness. Kindness doesn't flow from indulging all behaviours or always turning the other cheek.

In this book I'm thinking of kindness as something that's

done with the intention of benefitting someone else. Note the use of the word 'intention', because I'm sure we can all recall situations where we meant well, but our kindness didn't quite go as planned.

As well as asking participants in the Kindness Test about the kind acts that they carry out themselves, we also asked them about the kind acts they witnessed and where they took place.

TOP FIVE PLACES WHERE PEOPLE SEE KIND ACTS TAKING PLACE

1. At home
2. In medical settings
3. At work
4. In green spaces
5. In shops

The place where people told us they are least likely to see kind acts was online, which might not surprise you, given the bile and hatred we see on social media (although there is of course kindness and support there too – see more in Chapter 3½). But I was intrigued to see that the other places where kind acts were rarely witnessed were on public transport and in the street. The reason I was surprised about trains and buses is that I've been keeping a diary of the moments of kindness I observe when I'm out in public places. Again and again I see pushchairs carried up steps, seats given up for older people and dropped items returned to their owners. (Incidentally, alongside more results from the Kindness Test

I will be including some excerpts from my 'Kindness Diary' throughout the book and urging you to keep such a diary yourself.)

In the study, people were also asked to recall the last act of kindness that someone had done for them, and the last kind act they themselves had performed. Spreadsheets don't usually tend to have a big emotional impact on me, but I was genuinely moved, and will admit to the odd tear in my eye as I scrolled through thousands of short entries, each describing a moment of kindness between two people. There's evidence that we feel a warm glow when we do something nice for someone else – this glow shows up in brain scans. I definitely experienced such a glow just reading about the many kind acts and so between every chapter I've included a selection of these sentences, so that you too can share in this heartening experience.

It's good to receive as well as give

Before concluding this introduction, I want to touch on an area that is sometimes neglected when we consider kindness. Perhaps because it seems so obvious and therefore harder to find funding for, far less research time is devoted to the benefits to the recipient of a kind act, than to the giver. And yet we know from our own experience that being on the receiving end of kindness makes us feel cared for, cherished, heard, valued and above all, connected with other human beings. Those connections have a huge effect on our well-being. Psychological research demonstrates the difference that kindness and empathy can make to the way we develop as children, to our relationships throughout our lives and the way we cope in difficult times.[1] Kindness does have a positive impact on us. Here are just a few examples:

- Both adults and children rate their relationships as more satisfying if their parents or their partners are able to see things from their point of view.
- Likewise, people who feel kindly towards their partners are likely to have closer, more trusting relationships in the years to come.
- People who are empathic are less likely to worry obsessively when they are unhappy with something their partner has done, and more likely to forgive them.
- When students are asked to rate their lecturers, they value the lecturers' concern and consideration nine times more than their competence.
- Children with cancer experience less subjective pain if their parents respond empathically to them.[2]

It's obvious really, but it needs saying: we like it when people are kind to us.

A tale of two journalists

Twenty years ago or more, two famous journalists had their leaving do's at around the same time. One had a lavish party at a London club, with fine wine and fancy catering, all paid for by their employer. Hundreds attended, including the great and the good. Speeches were given lauding this journalist's achievements, which were considerable, but in huddles around the room many of the guests spent their time swapping tales of how awful this man had been to work with.

By contrast, the other journalist organised his own leaving party in a much humbler setting. There was a pay bar and guests chipped in for a buffet. No bigwigs came, but despite the event being on a Saturday night, people in their twenties, receptionists and cleaners, cheerfully turned up to give this sixty-something a good send-off. The talk all night was not of this man's professional achievements, though again they were considerable, but of what a thoroughly nice man he was.

I know, when the time comes, which leaving do I would rather have, and I hope that through reading this book you will wish to be remembered for being a kind person above all. For if that does turn out to be true, you will have enjoyed a happier and more fulfilled life, as well as a generous and giving one – and incidentally, there is no reason why it should hold you back from achieving other goals. You can be a top journalist – or even a famous rock star – and be kind to people at the same time. Kindness doesn't hold you back, it sets you free.

In an era of highly polarised opinion, in which even the phrase #bekind is at times weaponised on social media, and when the world faces such serious threats as armed conflicts, a refugee crisis, climate change and further pandemics, there is an urgent need for greater cooperation at the global, regional and societal level. And with anxiety, stress and depression on the rise, at a personal level too we need more focus on compassion and care. But for either of these things to happen, we need to recognise, appreciate and value kindness. Kindness helps us to forge connections with other human beings. It shouldn't be seen as incidental in our lives. It is a fundamental part of human nature. I hope, therefore, that *The Keys to Kindness* will unlock some of the mysteries of kindness and open doors to the ways in which we can all be kinder to each other, to the world and to ourselves.

LAST ACT OF KINDNESS RECEIVED

The Kindness Test

My friend tagged me in a post on Facebook describing me as pure sunshine – made me very happy.

I took my dog to a championship show, then struggled to erect my gazebo as it was very windy weather and three people, all women, rushed to help me.

My adult daughter painted my aging toenails before my niece's wedding.

My husband cleared up the pee our new puppy had done on the floor, even though we had an agreement that I'd do it.

I was unable to join friends in Cornwall for a week's holiday. They brought me back a Cornish goodie bag. Lovely thought.

My girlfriend kissed me. I'm really quite hideous.

My bird table fell to pieces and a friend, without telling me, made a new one from rescued wood which he treated and painted.

A friend listened to me telling a difficult story at length and gave advice and support.

Someone held a gate open so I could run through.

THERE IS MORE KINDNESS IN THE WORLD THAN YOU MIGHT THINK

Some years ago, a friend of mine tripped over the scooter her two-year-old son had abandoned in the street, cutting herself so badly that she was crying out in pain. Later she had to go to hospital to have stitches. An adult passer-by rushed to help her, but her son took no notice whatsoever. He was apparently unbothered by her suffering. He barely paused his tantrum.

This kind of story leads us to assume that toddlers are selfish little monsters, however much we might love them. Often it seems they simply don't *care* about anyone other than themselves and it's true that there is some evidence that toddlerhood is the time of life at which we are at our most aggressive and violent and that this soon subsides with age, leaving adolescents far more peaceable.[1] But there's a good reason why toddlers ignore others' pain or even cause it themselves. As thousands of psychological studies have shown, toddlers struggle to see another person's perspective, even if that person is their own mother. This is because their brains have not developed enough and their cognitive powers are limited. It's not really their fault they are so self-obsessed. But nor should we assume that little children are totally incapable of kindness.

The not-so-terrible twos

We've all seen a two-year-old refuse to share, holding a toy tightly to their chest, with a resolute determination that no other child will get to play with it. It takes children some time to learn to 'share nicely', a trait that, after all, not all adults are very good at practicing. Possession is a powerful feeling. Within psychology it's known as the endowment effect. We like to hold onto what is already ours and are reluctant to give it away or even to swap. In my earlier book, *Mind Over Money*, I covered some of the ingenious experiments devised to measure this effect.[2] For example, if you give someone a free mug, you'll find they're most unhappy to sell it back to you unless you give them more than its value, even though it was free in the first place. To have and to hold; that's our motto a lot of the time.

Given this is the case among us adults, what hope is there for toddlers? Well, as it turns out, the terrible twos are not quite so terrible after all when it comes to sharing. Or at least that is what a study by Julia Ulber and her team at the Max Planck Institute for Evolutionary Anthropology in the German city of Leipzig has shown.

Ulber started by giving pairs of two-year-olds a single bag of marbles. The toddlers were also shown a sealed box with a hole in it – and inside the box there was a xylophone. The researchers then demonstrated to the children that if a marble was posted through the hole in the box it landed on the xylophone, and the result was a loud jingling sound – the sort of sound that toddlers just love. Now, you might think that this scenario could only end in tears. There were only so many marbles in the bag and which toddler wouldn't grab all of them so that they could cause the maximum amount of xylophonic cacophony? The results though were more encouraging than you might imagine. True, in 19% of the trials one child did snatch all the marbles, leaving the other crying or having a strop. But this wasn't the full story or indeed the main finding. For in fact, almost half of the time the children – wait for it . . . divided the marbles between them equally.[3]

Now this might seem to many parents like the stuff of fantasy. But not only was this the result, things got better still. When the experiment was set up to be unfair, with one child receiving more marbles than the other at the start, a third of the children even handed some marbles over to the child who had lost out.

It is quite a remarkable result. But Ulber's work isn't some freakish outlier. It turns out that not only can toddlers be kind but, just like adults, they take pleasure in helping others – a reaction that, as I'll be arguing throughout this book, doesn't diminish the kindness shown, but deepens it.

Picture the scene of this next experiment. A researcher is hanging up some washing on a line using clothes pegs. Meanwhile a toddler is playing, rolling marbles into a tube which makes another of those fun noises. In due course the toddler runs out of marbles and the researcher runs out of clothes pegs, at which point the researcher takes a box from a windowsill and pretends to struggle to get its lid off. The toddler watches on. The box is then left on the floor, lid still on. The toddler, now without marbles to divert them, can't resist investigating the box and trying the lid, which of course – it's all a set-up – they can remove easily. Inside the box they find one of three objects: a piece of useless plastic, a marble or a clothes peg.

Now, all of these proceedings are captured on film so that the facial expressions and body language of the toddler participants can be analysed by the research team. And it is at this point in the experiment where the analysis becomes most interesting, because there are clear and measurable differences in how each child reacts, depending on which object they found in the box. If they found the useless piece of plastic, the toddler shows indifference, verging on disappointment. Finding the marble makes a child much happier of course. But it is when the children find the clothes peg in the box that they seem most pleased of all (in all but one instance, that is). The camera footage shows them walking over to the researcher with their chests puffed out with pride and smiles on their faces bigger even than the smiles of the toddlers who found a marble. It seems clear that they are delighted with a find which, after all, doesn't give them particular amusement, but which they've observed is helpful to the adult in hanging out the washing. It is, I must say, one of my favourite experiments in child psychology as the behaviour of these very small children is both very sweet and obviously kind.[4]

Mini Samaritans

So, contrary to popular belief, toddlers are capable of showing kindness through either sharing or helping. And when it comes to another type of kindness – comforting others – even younger children have been shown to demonstrate this behaviour.

For evidence of this, we go back to a study from the 1990s, conducted by a psychologist called Carolyn Zahn-Waxler at the National Institute of Maryland in the US. She trained mothers to fake distress in front of their one- to two-year-old babies and then to note down their observations of their children's responses. (To ensure that the mothers were not giving their little ones the benefit of the doubt too much, some of the mothers were videotaped.) The mothers either coughed or choked for ten seconds. Or they pretended to bump their foot or head, say ouch and rub it better. Or they displayed listlessness by sitting sighing for ten minutes. Or – most dramatically of all – they faked full-on sobbing for ten seconds. To add to the data, the mothers also noted how their babies behaved whenever similar incidents occurred naturally.

The reactions that Carolyn Zahn-Waxler and the mothers were looking out for were instances when the infants offered hugs, pats or kisses, or among the older ones who could talk, words of comfort or sympathy. Alternatively, the children might respond by whimpering or starting to sob themselves. What the study showed was that after their first birthday more than half the babies who were being followed showed a kind response of some sort at least once, initially hugging and patting. One-year olds responded sympathetically on 10% of occasions where the mother was upset. Not a huge percentage, but still notable. And by the time children had reached the age of two, they showed kindness an impressive 49% of the time.

What are we to make of these findings? First, that there is evidence that even one-year-olds can understand when their mother is distressed and respond by acting kindly towards her. But at the same time, being kind is hardly the default response of children at that young age. Remember my friend with the scooter injury. Indeed, there were occasions when the little ones did seem to enjoy their mother's apparent distress, particularly when they had caused the hurt themselves, though even this wasn't necessarily a sign of baby sadism, for as Zahn-Waxler speculated, some over-acting by the mothers may have given the incidents 'a comic quality'.[5] I have to admit this makes me really want to see those videos now.

Another influential researcher who takes an interest in altruism in infants is Michael Tomasello, who is also from the Max Planck Institute and was involved in some of the studies I described earlier. In one of his other experiments, Tomasello and a colleague found that toddlers as young as 18 months old will open a cupboard door for an experimenter when they see that the adult is carrying a stack of magazines that prevents them from opening it themselves.[6] The children tend to do this even if they are given a fun game to play, which they then have to abandon for a few moments if they wish to help. Moreover, the mini good Samaritans will go as far as to crawl over physical obstacles placed in their path, so deter-mined are they to assist the encumbered experimenters.

In another experiment, Tomasello and his colleagues involved small children in the task of opening a locked box with another person and found, strikingly, that while 42% of the toddlers helped an adult with the task, 75% of toddlers were prepared to help another toddler.[7] This suggests that little children are aware that another child of the same age is more likely to need some assistance, but also that they are being helpful without looking for something in return, since they might expect an adult to have more to offer. Their brains aren't developed enough to take the cognitive steps required to understand the concept of reciprocity. They are just being kind because they *are* kind. Their kindness is hardwired, part of the circuitry of being human, Tomasello argues. Incidentally, he has even found that chimpanzees who were fed by humans, but born in the wild, who tend to be better known for their aggression than their kindness, would hand an out-of-reach object to a human they had never seen before, without being given any bananas in return.

Tomasello refers to toddlers as 'indiscriminate altruists'. Rather sweetly, if they're going to be helpful, they'll do it for anyone. It's as they get older that children start to be more choosey. From an evolutionary perspective this makes sense. When we're very young we spend much more time with our own kin or with other trusted people, so we don't need to be as wary. As we get older, we encounter more and more unrelated people and start to make judgements and calculations about how to spread our kindness and who to trust.

Toddlers also care little for their reputation, whether it's for kindness or cruelty. Of course, they do enjoy getting praise from their parents, but they don't have an understanding of what other people think of them in general, rather than at that particular moment. They aren't able to comprehend the notion of adhering to social norms.

Growing kindness

As children get older, their understanding of kindness and their kindly acts become more sophisticated. This has been shown in the work of John-Tyler Binfet, a professor at the University of British Colombia, who is clearly a very kind man himself as among his other accomplishments is the development of a programme called BARK, which stands for Building Academic Retention through K9s (an acronym which must have taken a while to come up with!). BARK uses therapy dogs to support the well-being of stressed students on his college campus. When John-Tyler took part in Kindfest, a conference I was chairing online during the pandemic in 2020, he had a lovely support dog, a golden retriever, sitting beside him, which helped to relax all the participants and made for a great discussion. Anyway, John-Tyler's academic work on kindness starts with children drawing pictures of examples of their own kind actions.[8]

He finds that the acts fall into different categories, such as physical kindness and inclusive kindness, concepts that children only grasp when they get a bit older. In a drawing of physical kindness, for example, an eight-year-old girl depicted herself picking up a friend who'd fallen over. A drawing of inclusive kindness showed a girl crying and another asking why. The first girl says she has no one to play with, 'and so I played with her' the second girl said. In another drawing I liked – and which showed a quite complex insight into what can constitute an act of kindness – a boy had drawn a self-portrait of himself with huge ears as he worked in class. The boy explained he was 'helping my teacher by listening'.

Professor Binfet explained to the Kindfest audience that when he asked his young participants to draw examples of their teachers being kind he expected the pupils would depict scenes such as a teacher giving out sweets or offering the class extended break time. In other words, he thought the children would think of the acts which directly benefitted them. Instead, he was impressed to find that they were as likely to draw a teacher helping another student with their maths, say. And when ten- to eleven-year-olds wrote down their descriptions of kindness for him, they defined it as 'to make others feel included and happy'.

The children in the study were also asked to plan five kind acts for the coming week. They included in their lists acts such as helping a neighbour with his shopping and giving pizza to a brother. And there was one very sweet – and indeed highly thought-through – act that was mentioned. This boy would be careful not to mention his mum too much to his friend, he said, as the friend's mum had died the previous year. This showed both self-restraint and perspective-taking at an impressive level for a child so young.[9]

But if it's true that as children get older they get kinder, isn't it also true that they regress when they become teenagers? Well, yes, to some extent. Teenagers can be self-centred and inconsiderate (as well as surly and monosyllabic), but again it's not all their fault. For a start, it's difficult negotiating a path through puberty and towards independence, and neuro-scientific research from Professor Sarah-Jayne Blakemore (a big defender of teenagers) shows teenagers' brains, which are still developing, take longer to see things from another's perspective.[10] When assessing questions such as how a friend would feel if they weren't invited to your party, Professor

Blakemore, who is based at the University of Cambridge, found that adults could make judgements faster than adolescents and seemed to use their brains more efficiently. Not every part of the brain develops at the same rate as we grow up, so one theory is that the brain's reward system develops faster in adolescents than the prefrontal cortex, the part of the brain responsible for self-control and planning. This might explain why teenagers are sometimes more likely to make decisions that can seem selfish.

Despite this, John-Tyler Binfet of UBC has also found evidence that teenagers are certainly not hopeless cases when it comes to being kind. Just as he did with the younger children, he asked 14- and 15-year-old school students in Canada to plan five kind acts to accomplish across a week. He then categorised the acts they chose, with the most common involving helping someone (taking a crying classmate to the toilets, for example), followed by giving (offering another teenager a quarter for the vending machine, say) and then being respectful (which I was interested to see often consisted of *not* doing things – *not* being greedy at the dinner table, *not* teasing a sibling or friend).

I was also interested to see that there were no great differences between the kind acts boys and girls chose, except that more boys chose acts related to respect. This makes me wonder – perhaps because I'm biased towards my own gender – whether some of the girls might have taken it as read that you shouldn't do certain things, rather than defining restraint as an act of kindness. But perhaps that is hard on the boys. Overall, it's striking that the teenagers' ideas of what counts as kindness were quite nuanced and complex, such as cheering up a parent by loading the dishwasher, even though you hate doing it, or defending someone in a conversation even if you don't agree with their point of view.

Now, I can hear parents of teenagers saying at this point, this is all very well, but there's a BIG difference between a teenager *saying* they're going to do something and them *actually* doing it. Clearing away the clothes they've just tossed on their bedroom floor, for example. Or getting up before midday. Or *ever* doing anything other than playing computer games.

But again I want to defend teenagers. In fact, in this exercise, 94% of them succeeded in completing at least three of their planned kind acts and in total 943 kind acts were carried out by the 191 students, though it should be noted that the recipients of the kind acts were ten times more likely to be family or friends than a stranger.[11]

Too much shouldn't be made of these findings, of course – the teenagers were taking part in a staged exercise, after all. But even so, as Binfet himself argues, his work goes some way to challenging the most negative stereotypes around teenagers. The fact is they can be quite caring and considerate when they choose to.

Older and kinder?

We've seen that even little children and teenagers can be kinder than we think, but it is generally true that as we get older our capacity to be kind and our propensity to act in kind ways tends to increase. Of course, this is a generalisation and although some studies show that older adults are on average kinder than younger adults, others find no difference.

Also, many of these experiments involve tests of financial generosity or opportunities to gain financially if you act in a kind way, and that creates a problem. As I showed in my book *Mind Over Money*, the moment a situation involves money, we're put into a financial frame of mind which can skew our decision-making.[12]

To overcome this problem, a recent study examined how much physical effort people were prepared to exert in order to benefit someone else. Kind acts often involve physical exertion, whether it's helping a parent carry their pushchair up the station steps or running after a stranger who's dropped something, yet this type of kindness can get neglected in kindness research. Not in this study though – a study conducted by Patricia Lockwood from the University of Birmingham.

It involved people gripping a dynamometer, a device you hold in your hand and squeeze as tightly as you can. In this experiment, the harder and longer a person squeezed the device, which is quite hard work, the greater reward they could earn, sometimes for themselves and sometimes for others. So, what did Professor Lockwood's team find?

Well, in a nutshell, that older people demonstrated more kindness. More precisely, people aged between 55 and 84 would exert as much effort to win rewards for others as for themselves, whereas 18 to 36 year olds wouldn't.[13] Diving a bit deeper still, those in the younger group were prepared to put in a bit of effort to benefit others when this didn't involve too much exertion, but as squeezing the dynamometer got harder – there are six levels – they tended to wimp out, whereas the older people hung on in there. Not only that, but they reported feeling more of a warm glow after squeezing like mad for other people.

28

(And in case you're wondering, the research team did measure everyone's grip first to see how strong they were and took that into account, so the experiment took place on a level playing field, as it were.)

These findings aren't surprising. We know that the younger people are, the more cognitive biases they have towards looking out for their own interests, which could reflect their more precarious position just starting out in the world. This is not to say younger people aren't kind. In the Kindness Test age made only a tiny difference to how many kind acts people said they carried out and not nearly as much of a difference as personality (if you recall, extraverts, agreeable people and those who are more open to new ideas scored higher on average). Older people did say they donate more to charity though, and when people were asked how much of a surprise windfall of £850 they would give away, older people offered slightly more than younger people regardless of their income level.

As someone who is moving into 'middle youth', you might say, this evidence pleases me, as I'm looking forward to perhaps becoming kinder. And of course, I already have one advantage in the kindness stakes over, say, my husband, because I'm a woman and women are kinder than men, right?

Well, yes – sort of. On the whole, studies show that on average women score higher on tests of empathy and kindness (and they did in the Kindness Test too), though these findings may be the result of the way some studies were framed and the way men and women traditionally view themselves. Little girls – certainly when I was growing up – were encouraged to be the helpers, handed dolls to cuddle and care for and praised whenever we were kind and gentle. Boys, by comparison, were rewarded for showing strength and resilience, for being little tough guys. And maybe it's still happening. Just the other day someone sent me a picture of girls' pants in a shop with 'kind' written along the waistband, while the boys' equivalents had 'Hogwarts' and 'Xbox' on them. Small wonder then, that women tend to show more empathy than men, all things being equal. It's also possible that women feel more of a pressure to appear kind in such studies and so they take the trouble to act kindly while they're being watched or to tick all the boxes in questionnaires, claiming they do lots of kind acts and donate to charity.

Research conducted in 2008 changed that starting point by telling men that women are more attracted to sensitive men. Before their empathy was tested the men were told specifically that: 'Non-traditional men make better first impressions with women. In particular, they are seen as more interesting and easier to talk to, are judged to be more sexually desirable and more sophisticated at flirting, and are more likely to be in the company of women than men when leaving bars and clubs.' Now the wording here might sound rather dubious these days, but in terms of encouraging men to be more empathic in tests, it had the desired effect.[14] When men were told how desirable women found sensitivity, they became significantly better than other men at working out what other people were thinking and feeling. This suggests that our sense of whether or not it's valuable to be kind makes a difference to how we actually behave.

In another experiment, men and women were given a video to watch of a young woman who hadn't got the grades she needed to get onto a postgraduate course in the US. Similar to the previous study, the participants' task was to listen to her story and guess what emotions she might be feeling at certain points in the video. Women did better than men, until they were all offered money in exchange for correct answers. Then both men's and women's performance improved and the disparity between them disappeared.[15]

Here of course is a prime example of what I was talking about earlier – a financial incentive skewing results. But at the same time, the lesson could be that we can all be empathic, men just as much as women, the young just as well as older people, if we get the right motivation.

I'm certainly not suggesting that the route to a kinder world is that we should all get paid to be kind, but there's nothing wrong with praising kindness, rewarding it in other ways and above all encouraging it. We need to think how we can create a culture in which kindness is recognised and fostered more widely.

Looking for kindness amid the global gloom

I hope by now that I've cited enough credible research to convince you that it's not true that at any stage of our lives we are innately selfish and cruel or that acting in a kind way somehow goes against our nature. Rather, we start out quite kind (or as soon as we have the opportunity we do), and as we develop a range of relationships, as our brains mature and our ability to regulate our emotions grows, and if we get encouragement and support, we can and do become kinder still. That doesn't mean of course that everyone is kind or that any of us is kind all the time. It's just to say that kindness is an important element of our makeup and we are kinder than we sometimes give ourselves credit for.

One of the reasons we don't appreciate this fact is that negative personality characteristics tend to hog human attention, just as bad news predominates in news bulletins. And of course, we're right to be concerned about our propensity to demonstrate the so-called Dark Triad of personality traits – narcissism, Machiavellianism and psychopathy – as people who act on these traits cause a lot of pain and trouble, so we need to be on our guard against them in ourselves and in others.

But in fact, most of us, most of the time, are actually more driven by what the US psychologist Scott Barry Kaufman has dubbed the Light Triad of personality traits. These are Kantianism – that's to say treating people as ends unto themselves; humanism – in which we value the dignity and worth of each individual; and faith in humanity – where we believe in the fundamental goodness of humans.

(If you're interested, you can test yourself online for Light Triad traits.[16] It only takes a few minutes. I must say I found it quite reassuring that I scored 80% for my belief in the dignity and worth of each human and 75% for faith in humanity, triple what I scored on narcissism. Though, now I think of it, it is perhaps a little narcissistic to be boasting about these results, even though it turns out that I'm not at all unusual in scoring so highly.)

True, Kaufman's work is exploratory and it's still early days in this field of research, but his team also found that being a Light Triad sort of person is in our own interests, as people with those traits on average score their own quality of life highly. The fact is, taken as a whole, we humans are kinder than we often suppose – and we're not fighting against our dark natures, or acting against our selfish interests, when we act in kind ways.

A nice example of how kindness is innate in human beings can be found in an essay by the famous nineteenth-century writer, William Hazlitt. In the essay, Hazlitt recounts how he and the poet Samuel Taylor Coleridge were on a walk along the North Devon Coast near Lynton. They met a fisherman who told them that just the day before locals had tried to save the life of a drowning boy. The attempted rescue was at great risk to their own lives, but this didn't stop them. The fisherman's explanation for this behaviour was touchingly simple and heartfelt: 'Sir,' he told Coleridge, 'we have a *nature* towards one another.'[17]

But people do terrible things, I hear you cry. Look through history and around the world. Looks at what's happening right now. There is so much cruelty and wickedness. In addition to the horrors we see on the news, there are plenty of classic psychological studies to confirm the dimmest view of human behaviour. To take just two – now world-famous – examples, we apparently electrocute people just because we're told to and we stand by and do nothing when we are witnessing a brutal murder. Yet, as we will see, a closer look at these studies reveals inconsistencies in the way they've been reported in textbooks and a tendency to assume the worst, which is not backed up when the full picture is presented. It turns out that social psychology as an academic discipline has doubled-down on our negative view of humanity in a way that isn't justified by the facts.

In Stanley Milgram's famous experiment, for instance, a third of the participants refused point blank to give the man in the room next door a dangerous electric shock, even though the pressure on them to do so in the circumstances was enormous. Privately, Milgram came to the view that his study was more 'effective theatre' rather than 'significant science'.[18] Then, there's the notorious incident of Kitty Genovese who was murdered in 1964 in Queens, New York, when 38 people apparently saw what was going on and did nothing. In this case, most residents of the nearby block couldn't have seen what was happening and it turns out that the Assistant District Attorney only found half a dozen people who saw anything at all – and even then they were unclear about what was taking place.[19] So, still an appalling murder, but not quite as damning for the witnesses after all. Yet the story is so compelling that it's featured in plays, films and novels and it inspired the creation of the Guardian Angels, the volunteers who patrol the New York subway in red berets. There's even an episode of the TV show *Girls* called 'Hello Kitty' where the characters take part in an interactive theatrical version of her murder. It's true that classic psychological studies do display some evidence of our tendency to cruelty and indifference in some people in some situations, but they certainly don't prove that we are essentially selfish and inhumane.

At the global level, and looking back over the sweep of human history, two huge bestsellers of recent years – Stephen Pinker's *The Better Angels of Our Nature* and Rutger Bregman's *Humankind* – have piled up evidence to show that we humans can be, and increasingly are, decent, generous, caring and compassionate. Bregman's central contention is that of the Lynton fisherman: that humans are by nature kind – which is also the view of the philosopher Jean-Jacques Rousseau who argued that 'man is naturally good'. The evidence shows, Bregman argues, that primitive, nomadic tribes (our ancestors) were not violent or warlike and showed signs of being co-operative and friendly. And he cites the historian Professor Tine de Moor, from Erasmus University in Rotterdam, who has written: 'History teaches us that man is essentially a cooperative being, a *homo cooperans.*'

Pinker, whose monumental study came out a decade before Bregman's book, focuses on violence and it demonstrates, with an impressive weight of statistical evidence, that the era we are living in now is one characterised by high levels of peace and compassion. And in some ways I believe we continue to become kinder. In the nineteenth century or even the twentieth, would there be an outcry if a footballer kicked their cat?[20] I somehow doubt it. Where Pinker differs from Bregman is in his contention that 'we started off nasty and . . . the artifices of civilisation have moved us in a noble direction, one in which we can hope to continue'.[21]

He puts this down to humankind moving through six stages of progress, which he identifies as the Pacification Process, the Civilising Process, the Humanitarian Revolution, the Long Peace, the New Peace and the Rights Revolution. He also notes that 'a key insight of evolutionary psychology is that human cooperation and the social emotions that support it, such as sympathy, trust, gratitude, guilt and anger, were selected because they allow people to flourish in positive-sum games.'[22]

For the purposes of this book, the difference of view between Bregman and Pinker does not matter too much because they both agree – with masses of evidence to back up their views – that at this point in time our humanity is characterised not by war, violence, cruelty and selfishness, but the opposite. We are living in an era, perhaps an era we have never experienced before, in which we tend towards cooperation, civility, respect for others and indeed what Pinker terms 'the four better angels' of empathy, self-control, moral sense and reason. There is a dark side to our natures for sure, but it doesn't predominate in the way and to the extent we sometimes think.

My focus is more on the micro than the macro level, the personal rather than the global, but I'm also optimistic about the fundamental aspects of our much maligned (by us) species.

Of course, the negative is always salient and needs to be. We see bad things around us. And bad things are happening everywhere in the world. We've evolved to be alert to the possibility that a lion might emerge and eat us because – to use the language of a risk assessment – although the likelihood of this happening is low, the impact is certainly high. By comparison, a friend kindly offering to share their food is a high likelihood/low impact situation – so we take much less note of it.

Imagine I were to give you a timesheet to keep with you and asked you to keep a note of any emotions you experienced during the day, and the approximate time you felt them. Which kinds of feelings do you think would predominate? The answer, as you can probably guess, is the negative emotions such as sadness or anger or frustration. By contrast, if people are paged at random during the day and asked how they are feeling at that precise moment, much more contentment and happiness shines through. It is obvious when you think about it. How has your day been so far? I bet if you had a horrible row with somebody or you messed up a presentation at work that negative experience stands out much more sharply than the rest of the day, which was probably fine.

It's the same with kindness, I believe. We are generally quite kind to others and we generally receive kindness from others, but it is the fewer occasions when we are unkind or cruel that stand out, partly because they are more exceptional and partly because they rankle with us. I'd guess when you have been rude to someone, you spend much of the next few hours going '*Why* did I behave like that?'. But if you have just behaved in an ordinary, considerate way, you don't dwell on it. And if someone wrongs you, it's hard to let it go, but when someone is just nice to you, you might notice for a moment and then get on with life.

On top of this, our sense of ourselves as essentially kind is constantly challenged. If you live in a city, every day you will probably pass homeless people in the street and wrestle with whether it's right or wrong to give them money or – as we are increasingly urged to, not least by homeless charities – to walk on by. Maybe, like me, you smile weakly, apologetically at the person begging, trying through that smile to convey the complexity of the arguments. This might be termed – though not very pithily, I'll admit – as an I-give-regularly-to-one-of-those-homeless-charities-and-don't-feel-giving-cash-in-the-street-is-the-best-way-of-easing-your-situation-or-the-problem-in-general-but-I-sympathise-with-your-situation-nonetheless-and-incidentally-I-do-have-to-get-my-train-now-but-I-wouldn't-want-you-to-feel-that-I-am-heartless-or-that-I-am-ignoring-your-plight-or-devaluing-you-as-a-human-being-with-needs-and-qualities kind of smile.

Whether this registers with the homeless person I'm not sure. And if I'm honest, it doesn't make me feel any better.

But, as I say, many homelessness experts and those working most directly with homeless people tend to say that giving money to the street homeless isn't always a good idea. Your direct debit to a reputable charity with a track record of helping people into homes and rebuilding lives is both the more effective and the kinder action. Here, indeed, is an example of where planned, slightly arms-length kindness, turns out to be the more efficacious form of kindness than the random, spur-of-the-moment kindness.

In fact, we posed a not dissimilar scenario to people in the Kindness Test. They were told this: imagine you're going to the park to meet a friend for a picnic lunch. You are running late and being slowed down by the weight of your picnic basket, which contains a selection of items. On your way, you pass someone sat in silence on a bench close to the park entrance. The person is alone and looks thin and unkempt. You suspect they haven't had anything to eat for some time. You glance into your picnic basket and consider whether to share one or more items with the person. Bear in mind, you are already ten minutes late and the person is not making eye contact with you. As you approach or pass the person on the bench, it occurs to you that you could stop and offer them something from your picnic basket. What would you do?

The test revealed that people are much more prepared to show kindness to a stranger in this way than I would have predicted, with almost 70% of participants saying they would offer at least one item from their basket and more than a quarter saying they would invite the person to pick whatever they wanted. Even the people who were more wary explained that they were worried such a gesture might appear intrusive (this would have been my reaction) or that they preferred to donate in other ways or that they felt they should consult with their friend first. All in all, the results painted a picture of people as remarkably thoughtful and considerate and I take it as another example of humans being kinder than we often think.

On the other hand, in the Kindness Test we also asked participants whether they thought people had become kinder or not during their lifetimes. On this question, two thirds of respondents said levels of kindness had either remained the same or declined – a less optimistic finding. I immediately thought this must be explained by older people looking back with rose-tinted spectacles to the 'good old days', which they perhaps didn't remember as well as they thought. But, in fact, the data showed that age made very little difference to how participants responded to this question. Both young, old and in-betweeners tended to feel kindness levels had flatlined, if not gone down since they were born.

But what about the more recent past? For optimists, there is good news in the fact that two thirds of respondents in the UK thought that people had become kinder during the pandemic, perhaps a reflection of communities pulling together through the lockdowns. But then, in North America a sizeable minority thought people had become *less* kind since Covid-19 took hold of our lives, maybe because polarisation in the US over vaccination and mask-wearing was particularly bitter. As is often the case with data, the results aren't always straightforward.

When you look across all the studies conducted in the US into kindness in the last forty years, a similarly mixed picture emerges.[23] The bad news is that by some measures empathic concern, trust and civic engagement have declined during that time. But then, charitable giving, volunteering and tolerance have increased. So, depending on what measure you take and how you ask the questions, a different conclusion about humanity can be drawn.

I want to end this section on a high note, though, by going back to a question from the Kindness Test that I mentioned earlier. That question is: if you had an unexpected windfall of £850, how much, if any, of it would you give away? The average amount was £252 – almost a third. This wasn't actual money of course; the situation was hypothetical. Perhaps in reality, people would give less – or none at all (and I have to add that even in the test more than three times as many people said they'd give away none of the money, than all of it). But even so, the research team was impressed with the generosity on display. At the very least, the impression we sometimes have of ourselves that we are all selfish and grasping is often a false impression. There's a good side that we need to notice, nurture and encourage.

Contagious – in a good way

Whether or not we have become kinder over the last few years, in the sweep of history, things are looking up. And there's another reason why human beings might be getting kinder as time goes on: because kindness is contagious. Now I realise that we are sensitive to the word 'contagious' after living through Covid-19, but trust me, what I'm about to set out here is an example of a pandemic we should all welcome – one in which kindness begets kindness begets kindness – and so it goes on.

Many different lab studies have found that people who receive kindness, go on to carry out a kind act themselves, sometimes through directly returning the favour, but also by being kind to someone else. One example I like is a study by a psychologist in the US called Monica Bartlett which was conducted back in 2006.

All the participants in this study were first required to take part in a 'tedious and repetitive exercise' on a computer which nonetheless required a lot of concentration. Having completed the task, half of the participants were then shown an episode of the American comedy show *Saturday Night Live*, ostensibly as part of a small follow-on task, but actually to put them in a better mood. Meanwhile, the other half suddenly saw their screens go blank. They were told a technician had been called and would come to fix the computer, but there was a chance their scores had been lost and they'd have to do the whole exercise all over again. They, of course, were less than happy bunnies. But then someone ostensibly taking part, but in fact an accomplice in the research team, said they'd try to fix the computer, which of course they succeeded in doing, thereby retrieving the lost scores, much to the relief of all concerned. Afterwards, all of the people taking part in the study were asked if they'd be willing to do a favour and fill in some quite dull paperwork.

You might expect that the people who'd been put in a better mood by watching the comedy show would have been the more amenable. But no, it was the other half of the participants who persisted for longest with the paperwork. Why? Well, because to do so was a way of 'paying forward' the kindness shown to them by the person who fixed their computers and saved them from having to repeat the first exercise.[24]

The concept of paying it forward was around for a long time before it got its name. One of its earlier advocates was Benjamin Franklin, a Founding Father of the United States, who helped to draft the Declaration of Independence. Franklin was also the inventor of the lightning rod and bifocal glasses, as well as being a writer, publisher, printer, scientist . . . the list of his achievements goes on and on. In 1784, Franklin wrote a letter to a merchant called Benjamin Webb, who, facing bankruptcy, had fled to Switzerland.[25] Webb, it seems, was a friend of Franklin's grandson and so Franklin agreed to lend him some money. But there was a condition. Franklin didn't want to be repaid directly. Instead:

> . . . *when you meet with another honest Man in similar Distress, you must pay me by lending this Sum to him; enjoyning [sic] him to discharge the Debt by a like operation when he shall be able and shall meet with such another opportunity – I hope it may thus go thro' many hands before it meets with a Knave that will stop its Progress. This is a Trick of mine for doing a deal of good with a little money.*[26]

Even if you struggle at first with the Ye Olde Englishe (albeit with an American accent), I'm sure you get the point: Franklin didn't want Webb to pay him back, he wanted him to help someone in the future who got into debt. We don't know if Webb complied with Franklin's exhortation or proved to be the dastardly 'Knave', but Franklin was onto something – and it is an idea through which kindness can proliferate.

Two hundred and thirty years later, researchers in the US stood in a subway station looking for people who might be prepared to help them in an experiment. If people agreed to participate, the researchers led them to a nearby bench to play the dictator game. This might sound rather ominous, but in fact the game doesn't involve invading other countries or executing political opponents. Rather it is about making a decision to pass on money to another person or not. The sum each 'dictator' was given was the princely amount of $6. They could keep the lot, give it all away, or keep some and give some away to the next player (who they didn't know), in whatever proportion they chose. The next person was then told how much the previous player had left them and asked how much of an additional $6 they would like to pass on to the next person. And so on.

It probably won't surprise you to learn that if the previous player had been greedy and kept all or most of the $6, then the subsequent player was more likely to be greedy too and not to share the money fairly, while if they were given all the money, they passed on an average of $3.71, so not the whole amount. They did pay it forward, but not completely. The authors conclude that this shows that 'greed prompts greed'.[27] Which is certainly one way of looking at it – and a somewhat depressing finding. But the study also showed the opposite effect, for when a previous player received $3 initially (i.e. the previous person had shared it equally), they left the next person an average of $3.38, slightly *more* than half. And this is striking I think: the players left nothing by the previous player, nonetheless chose to pass on at least some of the additional money they received – on average $1.32. Not a huge amount perhaps, but not to be sneezed at.

Incidentally, when the experiment was repeated, but this time the amount received by a player was based on rolling a dice, they were inclined to be less generous to the next player than when they thought a real person had left the money for them. In this iteration of the game, the amount received was, it seems, seen as a chance win, something it was legitimate to hang onto, with no questions of reciprocity involved. Because no human-to-human kindness was shown in the first place, the paying-it-forward effect was weakened.

So far, we've been considering examples where an act of kindness by one individual prompts not direct reciprocity, but an act of kindness from the receiver towards *another* beneficiary. In other words, a chain of kindness between individuals is created. This undoubtedly results in a prolifer-ation of kindness, through a sort of domino effect, but it doesn't spread kindness exponentially.

That can happen though through the influence that social norms have on our behaviour. If we hear that other people, especially people we identify with, are behaving in a certain way, then it's been shown we're more likely to behave in that way too. We don't have to have met any of these people, we just have to be convinced they did something – in this case, a kind or thoughtful thing – and we are more inclined to do it ourselves.

In the now classic study of the power of social norms carried out by the American psychologist Robert Cialdini and his colleagues, a notice was put up in hotel bathrooms telling people that the majority of guests chose to reuse their towels for the good of the environment. This simple technique resulted in most people thereafter keeping their towels rather than asking for them to be replaced with fresh ones.[28] As a result, this practice is now standard in hotels around the world, and has of course saved huge amounts of water and energy.

So social norms can help us to become kinder to our planet and indeed kinder to each other without the need for direct human contact. But even so, we all like person-to-person interactions and in this next example the persuasive power of human beings who practise what they preach was shown to really work.

In 2012 a campaign began called 'Solarize Connecticut'. Volunteers from 58 different towns in the US state signed up as 'Solar Ambassadors' and went door to door trying to persuade people to have solar panels installed on their roofs in order to help the environment.[29] Of course, all the volunteers were enthusiastic about this green way of bringing energy to people's homes, but as you might expect, some volunteers were more successful than others. Yes, those who had solar panels on their own roofs recruited 62% more new members to the scheme than the volunteers who didn't. This is because they were able to answer 'yes' to the 'well, if it's so good, have you done it yourself?' question. Here again we have an example of people being influenced to do a good thing, in this case for the environment, by a person who had already acted that way themselves. It shows, I think, that we all have a natural propensity to be kind and considerate, but we are particularly motivated to act in this way by examples of others doing so.

Become a kindness twitcher

One way we can come to appreciate the kindly side of our nature is to become what could be called a kindness twitcher. Just as a bird spotter goes out to look for birds and keeps lists of what they see, we could be more on the alert for instances of kindness, both in our own actions and the actions of others, so that kindness becomes more salient in our lives.

The positive psychologist Martin Seligman has demonstrated that if before you go to bed you write down three things, however small, that made you happy during the day, your levels of general happiness will gradually improve. The reason for this is not only that it gives you something nice to think about before you try to get to sleep, but that noting positive moments becomes such a habit that you soon start looking out for them during the day. This was so useful to me during lockdowns.

I've found that something similar happens with kindness. Not surprisingly, in the Kindness Test the amount of kindness that people said they observed varied. Taking the global results as an example, people observed kind acts taking place most often if they lived in Africa, followed by North America, while in Europe the figures were slightly lower. Yet when we asked people how much kindness they *personally* received, the scores were more similar, regardless of where people lived. Similarly, older people across the world said they saw less kindness around them and yet they received plenty. How are we to explain these discrepancies? One answer may be that kind acts are taking place, and yet some people in some places are not as attuned to noticing them and only see them when they're very obvious.

So just as some people keep gratitude diaries of the things they are thankful for, I think we should all start keeping a Kindness Diary. I've done it myself and I've discovered that the more I look out for kindness, the more I notice it. Here's an excerpt from my diary.

Wednesday 9.35 a.m.
At the station there's a woman quite far ahead of me with a pushchair. The man behind her offers to help and attempts to carry the pushchair up the stairs, but it's going wrong. As well as the small child, the buggy is loaded with shopping and it's too heavy. By now they're on the steps, so it's too late to put the buggy down. He calls out that he's struggling. I'm too far behind, but a v. smiley woman helps. They get to the top of the steps, and the buggy owner and two helpers all look delighted to have succeeded together, as a team.

Saturday 2.30 p.m.
Walking along my street. There's a table with plates of cakes and biscuits – clearly homemade. Two little girls are selling them to raise funds for Ukrainian refugees. All within days of Russian troops moving into Ukraine.

Monday 6.40 p.m.
On a packed train in London. There are dings as the young man standing next to me receives messages on his phone. He looks around him, scanning the faces of all the masked people in the carriage and starts typing. More dings. Then another man squeezes past a few people and says to Man no. 1 'Is it you?' Now I'm intrigued. I

want to know what's going on. 'Yes,' he says and hands over a wallet. Man no. 2 is thrilled and thanks him again and again. During a five minute journey, the first man has found a wallet, worked out who it belongs to, contacted him and returned it. They do a quick fist bump. Despite their masks I can see their eyes crinkling with happiness. It's rather lovely.

I kept the diary as an experiment, but I haven't stopped noticing kind acts taking place and I hope I don't. When we look out for it and tune into it, kindness is there, every day. And sometimes we are the ones carrying out the kind acts, probably more often than we think.

LAST KIND ACT CARRIED OUT FOR SOMEONE ELSE

The Kindness Test

I helped a friend who has dementia find her way home.

I allowed my partner to sleep longer, then made him coffee before he took over looking after our newborn.

A cyclist in front of me just keeled over. I went to check if he was OK. He was semi-conscious and I waited to help him up.

I checked in with a friend who is giving up smoking.

I gave a hungry man £20.

The carnival in Leeds on bank holiday Monday has been cancelled due to Covid again. So I made my partner jerk veg and rice and peas.

I bought from a charity shop and intentionally overpaid.

I read to my wife over breakfast from a book we're reading together.

A shop assistant was being sworn at and was upset, so I went over to support her.

Does it have to be 'someone'? Do animals count? Twice a day I feed all my local birds and squirrels.

I gave the pencil back.

2

BEING KIND MAKES YOU FEEL GOOD AND THAT'S OK

At the end of each day, Ursula Stone, a florist who lives and works in New Barnet in north London, goes around her local supermarkets and picks up flowers which have passed their sell-by date. Blooms that would otherwise be thrown away are used to create low-cost bouquets that are affordable for places such as care homes, as well as for individual customers on low incomes. Ursula also provides training and employment for former young offenders, giving them the chance of a better life in the future. If all this were not enough, she also 'flower bombs' public places, leaving bouquets with notes saying, 'Please take these, they're for you to enjoy'.

Bernadette Russell is an author, blogger and campaigner, who for the last decade has made it her mission to spread kindness around her community and beyond. Among her many kind acts – she performs one every day – is decorating phone boxes and leaving pound coins in them, suggesting people use the money to call someone they love.

Most of the time neither Ursula nor Bernadette sees the results of their generosity and good heartedness. They don't know who's going to use the prettified phone boxes or pick up the bouquets of flowers left in the park. But even so, they'd be the first to admit that they gain something personally from their actions. Not something financial or practical. No, the gain is purely emotional. It is that warm glow of satisfaction that comes from acting in a kind way to others.

If we're the recipient of kindness, it's obvious that we benefit. We feel valued and cared for, and when the kind act comes from a stranger, we're reminded that there is more humanity in the world than we sometimes think. But I want to examine the multiple benefits that also accrue to the purveyors of kindness. Because while behaving compassionately improves the lives of others, it also improves our own lives. There are measurable boosts to health, both mental and physical. Behaving kindly can act as a buffer against burnout and stress – and improve our well-being. It brings us happiness and can even help us to live longer.

These are big claims, and it is important to qualify them by saying that sometimes the benefits we experience from being kind aren't large. But they are nonetheless real and backed up by solid evidence. Let's start at the offices of Coca Cola in Madrid.

Win/win – why kind acts are a real double whammy

These offices were the setting for a study devised by psychologists at the University of California Riverside. The researchers randomly assigned people who worked for the soft drinks company to become either the bestowers or the recipients of kind acts.[1] The first group – the bestowers – were told that as part of a study into happiness in the workplace, each week for four weeks they would be asked to plan and perform five acts of kindness at work in a single day. They were given new examples to motivate them each week. Acts didn't have to be large; bringing someone a drink, sending a thank you email, or cheering up a colleague who was having a bad day. The acts should be aimed at anyone on a list of ten colleagues they were given. Meanwhile, the second group – the receivers – who didn't know what the first group was up to, were asked to count up any generous acts that they noticed taking place in the office.

Before the study began, everyone taking part, including a control group, completed questionnaires to assess their mood, their feelings about their job and their life satisfaction. And each week, and then a month and three months after the kind acts started, the staff filled in the questionnaires again. This allowed the researchers to see what impact the kind acts were having and how long any benefits might last.

The initial results showed that from these small acts alone the two groups experienced increases in both job and life satisfaction. But interestingly, a month on, the bestowers felt better about both their jobs and their lives, while the gains in satisfaction for the receivers had worn off. And remember, the bestowers were not necessarily that kindly in their ordinary lives; they'd been instructed and directed to be kind, perhaps contrary to their usual nature. Even so, being kind gave them a personal boost that lasted longer than the boost felt by the recipients of their acts.

Not, I should add incidentally, that the longer-term impact on the recipients wasn't considerable – in a different way it was in fact even more impressive. For the study found that those on the receiving end of the kind acts in the office performed three times as many kind acts for others in the follow-up period than they did before the experiment. That's quite a finding. It underlines once again, as we saw in Chapter 1, that kindness can be contagious.

Next I want you to imagine you've just been stopped in the street and given free money. Would you predict that it would make you happier to treat yourself to something nice with it, or to treat someone else? Most people predict the former. After all, happiness comes from indulging ourselves, doesn't it? Well, yes, in certain circumstances. But it turns out being generous to someone else can bring us even more satisfaction.

One morning, people walking down a street in the Canadian city of Vancouver were asked to take part in an experiment run by the American psychologist Elizabeth Dunn. If they agreed, they were given an envelope containing either a $5 or $20 bill, along with some instructions. Half the people were told to spend the money on themselves and to do so by the end of the day. The other half were instructed to give the money to charity or to use it to buy a present for someone else. That evening, the researchers spoke to all the participants. The first group said they'd bought a variety of things for themselves, such as earrings, sushi or coffees. People from the second group bought toys for children, gifts for friends or gave the money to homeless people in the street. Then the researchers asked each participant to rate their mood.

Whether they'd received five dollars or twenty made no difference to a recipient's mood score, nor did what they'd bought with the money. What mattered was *who* they'd spent their money on. The people who had spent it on someone else felt significantly happier than those who treated themselves.[2]

The German philosopher Friedrich Nietzsche famously exclaimed: 'He who cannot give anything away cannot feel anything either.' I take it to mean that only by making some sacrifice can we be in touch with our true selves. Nietzsche seems to suggest that a certain selflessness and generosity to others is essential to our own well-being and recent research has borne out the truth of this observation.

One study, published in 2013, using Gallup World Poll data from a randomly selected, nationally representative sample of people in 136 different countries, found that those who say they've donated to charity that month have, on average, higher levels of well-being, than people who haven't.[3] This was irrespective of income level and so, in some cases, donating to charity must have deprived people of money they needed for themselves. Even so they felt better for making the sacrifice.

Another study which tracked large numbers of people in the US over many years, showed that the more cash people donated as a proportion of their income, the higher their levels of well-being. And although this may seem extraordinary, the impact was still evident a whopping *nine* years later.[4] Now the effect was modest, but it did remain even when well-being, physical health, income, education and religiosity were taken into account.

The psychologists Silvia Morelli and Jamil Zaki found some similarly interesting effects in their studies of kindness among friends.[5] Their research involved emailing pairs of friends at 5 p.m. every day for a fortnight and asking each person to record how many kind things they'd done for their friend that day. Morelli and Zaki also asked the participants how much empathy they felt for their friend that day and how they were feeling themselves. As you might have guessed by now, on the days when one friend had helped the other, the well-being of the kindly friend was higher. And this feeling of satisfaction lasted into the next day as well, chiming with the studies we saw earlier. The impact was notably strong if the issue the friend had helped with resonated for them, giving them a special emotional connection to their friend. So, if they listened to them talk about a relationship breakup when they'd been through something similar, then helping had an even more positive effect on them.

In these cases, the high level of empathy drove an emotional engine, adding meaning and joy to the acts of kindness. Developing empathy, Morelli and Zaki argue, is a vital first step towards becoming kinder and in turn experiencing well-being through acts of kindness. (This is a subject we will be returning to later in Chapter 5.)

In the Kindness Test there was a clear association between kindness and feeling good. People who regularly receive lots of acts of kindness have higher levels of well-being. But the study also found that people who carry out more kind acts have higher levels of well-being on average (and incidentally, just noticing other people carrying out kind acts also boosts well-being). Now remember this was a snapshot in time. We didn't follow people for five years tracking how many acts of kindness they performed, along with their well-being, all the time looking for patterns (although that's a study I'd love to see), so we can't be sure which came first. It's possible that the people who had the highest levels of well-being were in a better position to carry out kind acts because they felt good about themselves to start with. But the weight of evidence heavily suggests that acting in a kind way leads to increased well-being rather than the other way round.

There are of course different types of well-being that result from different outlooks and lifestyles. The Ancient Greek philosopher Aristippus who founded the Cyrenaic school of philosophy, emphasised hedonic well-being. In his view the goal of life is to have as many pleasurable moments as possible through immediate sensory experience. Less than a hundred years later, Aristotle focused more on eudaimonia, the kind of well-being that results from fulfilling your potential, achieving the best that you can in life and, crucially, considering those achievements worthwhile – or as Aristotle put it, 'activity of soul exhibiting virtue, or if there are more than one virtue, in accordance with the best and most complete'.[6] Acting kindly plays into this second, eudaimonic type of well-being whereby the sense of satisfaction a person experiences derives from them feeling that life has meaning and purpose.

Most of us, of course, do not live our lives according to one school of philosophy or another. Rather we mix and match. So, much as we might like a nice meal in a fancy restaurant or a lovely foreign holiday, few of us would feel fulfilled if that was all our lives consisted of. We balance immediate, selfish pleasures with work, family and social obligations, which may sometimes be a grind at the time, but which give us satisfaction in the longer run. Altruism tends to fall into this category of pleasure, as indeed the philosophers of the Cyrenaic school acknowledged.

But even if we all accept that bestowing kindness can increase our own well-being, there remains the question of how *much* of a difference such acts can make. You may give to a range of charities, volunteer at a local foodbank or homeless shelter, and generally act kindly towards others, but can the satisfaction you get from these activities outweigh dysfunctional relationships, a job you dislike, poor health and precarious finances? Surely, performing kind acts can't really compensate if everything else in your life feels as if it's going wrong?

Well, no, it can't – is the short, and perhaps not surprising, answer to these blunt questions – as Oliver Scott Curry, from the University of Oxford, has shown. He brought together all the best studies on this topic from around the world – mainly from Europe and North America, but also from South Africa, South Korea and Vanuatu, an archipelago of 83 islands in the South Pacific. He then aggregated the data to produce a major meta-analysis. And what he found from all this work was that behaving kindly has what's described in statistical terms as a 'small to medium effect' on our well-being.[7] In other words, performing lots of kind acts doesn't, as some of the more overexcited kindness bloggers sometimes claim, transform a miserable life into an ecstatic one. But at the same time, Scott Curry's findings do suggest that acting in kind ways has as much impact on a person's well-being as mindfulness, say, or positive thinking, where the focus is more directly on the self. And generally, any shift in well-being is notoriously difficult to achieve, so anything that makes even a small difference is worth having. Moreover, the highest quality studies into the effect of acting kindly show the largest boost to personal well-being, suggesting that the impacts Scott Curry found from his meta-analysis could be on the conservative side.[8]

More intriguingly, to feel the benefits of your own kindness, you don't have to be kind all the time. A study in 2021 found that simply recalling one of your past acts of kindness had as much of an impact on your well-being as carrying out a new act. Now I should point out immediately that the authors of this study are keen to stress that the takeaway from their study is not to rest on your kindness laurels, because of course if you stop acting kindly you won't be building up that bank of kind memories to recall in the future.[9] Even so, it goes to show how the warm glow we get from acting in a kind way can be long lasting. The embers burn for some time, adding more fuel to my argument that being a kind person is also to be a happy – or at least, a happi*er* – person.

And one final thing in this section. Neuroscientific research has revealed why we feel this warm glow when we act in kind ways. There are reward centres in our brain connected by what is known as the mesolimbic pathway. These areas become active when we see someone we love, for example, or are given some chocolate or some money. But they are also stimulated by something else – and that is giving something away to another person. Even more than that, it's been found that some parts of the brain such as a region called the subgenual anterior cingulate cortex, seem to be activated more when we give away money than when we receive it.[10] So kindness is not contrary to our nature. Our brains reward us for it.

The joys of volunteering

So far, I've talked mainly about the benefits that accrue to the giver if a person spends money kindly, or gives to charity, or carries out small acts of kindness in everyday life. But there is a more formal type of kind act, practised by millions of people around the world, one many millions more rely on, and that is volunteering.

One of the obvious advantages of volunteering as an act of kindness is that it brings a volunteer into contact with other people and connects them with their wider community. There is a really strong social element to this type of kindness which brings added benefits to people who practise it; benefits that can be life-changing.

When Amina was growing up in the Democratic Republic of Congo, she lived with her family in a large, guarded compound, with a monkey and a parrot as her pets. The guards were there to protect her and her siblings because Amina's rich merchant father was a man of such status that he was in effect the king of the region. There were servants, there were huge communal meals every night, people constantly coming and going. Amina was driven to school in an SUV. It was a luxurious and happy life, fit for a tribal princess.

But only a few years later, Amina was in the Ivory Coast, sleeping on the floor under the bar where she worked, having fled from the DRC. She had witnessed and been subjected to terrible violence, her parents were almost certainly dead, and she had no idea where her siblings were. She was alone, scared and vulnerable.

Fast-forward a few more years, and Amina was woken at dawn by security guards as she lay huddled and freezing in a phone box in Croydon in South London. The phone box was outside the government building where she was required to register for asylum. She'd been told she had to phone ahead to get an appointment, but the pay phone had swallowed her only coin before she could make the call. Yet again she had to restart her life with nothing.

Depression followed, and a spell in a psychiatric inpatient unit where her long hair was so full of lice that it had to be cut off. Amina was referred to a charity whose experts helped her to come to terms with the traumas she had experienced. Other specialist agencies and refugee support groups helped her to rebuild her life to the point at which she now has a secure home where she lives with her daughter and baby son, has got a degree, a job, has set up her own business and is studying for an MBA.

Why am I telling you this story, the story of a remarkable woman who I'm privileged to count as a friend? Well, while Amina goes out of her way to say how grateful she is for the help she has received herself, when people ask her how she has coped with so many tragedies and traumatic experiences, she answers that it was helping others that got her through. Only by volunteering to assist other asylum seekers through the Refugee Council and other charities has she been able to survive and then transform her own life. Her voluntary work gave her something to look forward to. She says the knowledge that she was making a small difference to other people returned meaning to her life. It made so much of a difference to her that a pause in her volunteering while there was less to do one Christmas, led to such a great deterioration in her mental health that she was admitted to hospital. After she began to recover she told the doctor she wanted to leave so that she could continue volunteering. She was discharged from hospital the same day.

Obviously, this is an exceptional example of how volunteering can benefit not only the people being helped, but the helper themselves, yet Amina's experience is one that is shared, in less dramatic ways, by countless others. Take the experiences of an unusual group of people who lived in the former East Germany.[11] I describe them as unusual not because of their own personality traits, but because they were closely studied every year for a relatively long period of time – 1985 to 1999 – a period that spanned the reunification of Germany. When the research team first started following them, the participants lived in a highly controlled, communist state, then after the fall of the Berlin Wall in 1989, they experienced rapid change, as they became citizens of a free, democratic and capitalist country. Some aspects of their lives were better under the new system, some weren't. It can still come as a surprise to people in the West, that despite the freedoms and generally greater prosperity, on average, life satisfaction for residents of the former East Germany dropped after reunification. One change that partly explains this reaction concerned volunteering. In the former East Germany voluntary work was common, and many sports clubs and societies were attached to public companies. Volunteering was encouraged and demonstrated that you were a good citizen and a loyal party member, which could bring its own advantages. But after the Wall fell, the infrastructure for volunteering began to collapse, and some organisations ceased to exist, while others remained. More than 37% of the people in this longitudinal study who had volunteered in the GDR, were no longer able to do so. This provided the chance to see what a difference volunteering made to people, in what's referred to in psychology as a natural experiment. Among this group there was a notable drop in life satisfaction compared with those who were still able to volunteer in the old ways or had found new volunteering opportunities. Of course, it's possible that it was unhappiness about other things, rather than the absence of volunteering in their lives, that led some in the first group to feel dissatisfied. But the authors did carefully control for feelings of insecurity. All in all, this study suggests that even when people might have volunteered because they had to be seen to do so, it still gave them considerable satisfaction and when the opportunity was not there to volunteer that sense of satisfaction declined.

Of course, the motivations a person has for volunteering vary. One study of volunteers between the ages of 19 and 76 at five hospices in the Midwestern and Western United States, found that the younger volunteers were more motivated by the prospect of meeting new people in their community, while the older people wanted to be of service, or felt a sense of obligation to their community.[12] Which might make you think that older people have slightly more noble intentions than young people. Until that is, you look at the research which shows that older people are among those who have been shown to benefit most from volunteering in terms of enhanced well-being. This is because volunteering can give them back that sense of self-worth, identity and purpose that might have come with their previous roles at work or as a parent. A large longitudinal study was conducted in a Florida retirement community, involving people who were over the age of 72, but didn't need any extra assistance. At the start of the study the research team measured mood, depressive symptoms and life satisfaction among the elderly participants. They measured the same things at the end of the study three years later.[13] The results are interesting because they're more nuanced than you might expect.

Almost half of the elderly people volunteered in a formal

capacity during the three years and at the end of the study their mood scores were found to be significantly higher than those of people who didn't volunteer. This was true even when the research team controlled for factors that could inhibit volunteering, such as health and disability, and whether participants could drive themselves around. There was though a notable caveat in this study which goes to show there are limits to the positive effects of volunteering on a person's well-being. There was no difference in depressive symptoms between participants in the study who volunteered and those who didn't. This finding suggests that while volunteering can give a person a boost, the effect is not strong enough to counter serious mental health issues.

Still, if you want to live longer, you could do worse than volunteer. That's the conclusion of a meta-analysis of several different studies.[14] Indeed, the risk of dying is almost *halved* in those who volunteer compared with those who don't.

Now, just one minute, I can hear you saying. That is quite a claim, shouldn't we treat it with considerable caution? And yes, there is an obvious difficulty in trying to study the relationship between volunteering, physical health and life expectancy. After all, it is only healthy older people who are able to go out and volunteer at their local charity shop or community centre. Anyone who is so ill that they can't leave the house, will find it much harder, if not impossible, to do so. These older people may well not live as long, but how do we know that isn't due to the illness or frailty that's stopping them volunteering in the first place?

Responsible researchers are wise to just these sorts of issues and the best studies certainly do take into account fitness at the start of the study. So, in the meta-analysis I've just mentioned, once the researchers controlled for health, age, sex and whether people were employed or not, the risk of dying during the period of a study among those who volunteered wasn't halved. *Aha!* I hear you cry. But, wait for it. It was still cut by a quarter, which, by any standards, is an impressive finding.

Incidentally, if there was a religious aspect to the volunteering the effect was stronger still. Which may or may not explain why the ladies who do the flowers at the parish church seem to live forever.

More than well-being

This last study shows that acting in a kind way to others does more than increase a person's general sense of self-satisfaction in a nice, but fuzzy way. The warm glow can radiate out to improve physical and mental health.

One study conducted in the Chinese city of Jinan found that even just thinking about kind acts they'd performed made people physically stronger, induced them to walk faster and made heavy weights feel lighter.[15] The effects were only temporary, but nonetheless intriguing, so let me tell you how they did it.

In one section, one group of participants were first asked to think of a time they had helped someone (who wasn't a relative) and to tell that story. Meanwhile a second group – and they drew the short straw I guess – spent the time preparing for an exam. Then both groups were given dumbbells and told that for every 30 seconds they could lift the weights, they would be given a free gel pen. The weight of the dumb-bells was the same for both groups and so was the prize, so the only way to explain why the first group could hold the dumb-bells for longer than the second group was that they'd been given a physical boost by recalling their acts of kindness.

Convinced? In other elements of the study, participants had to remember an occasion when they had spent money on someone else, or imagine when they might do so in the future. Afterwards they were timed walking along a corridor or, alternatively, they had to hold a box and guess its weight. Again, the group who had kindness in mind were quicker at the walking exercise than the control group and they believed the box was lighter than the control group did. The researchers concluded from this that a sense of their own kindness was making participants both faster and stronger.

Now I love the idea that this might have been the reason for their success. But I would treat it with some caution because it is an example of something known within psychology as priming, where participants are made to think about a particular subject and that in turn influences what they do next. These studies have been controversial because they haven't always been easy to replicate. Even so, there could be something going on here, even if it is just a case of a person who reflects on their kindness getting a slight boost which temporarily increases their energy levels.

It leads me to wonder if the reason Usain Bolt was so fast at the 100 metres was because, as he settled into the blocks, he recalled the times he'd sent his mum a bunch of flowers. And maybe those powerlifters who can 'clean and jerk' absurd weights are energised by the large donation they made the previous week to a children's hospice. Fanciful perhaps, but isn't it nice to speculate that thinking about our own kindness could give us superpowers?

Back in the real world, we're on safer ground in stating that acting kindly has a greater impact on your psychological well-being than on your physical health.

And it should also be said that most of these studies involve people who are on the whole in good health. But what if you deliberately asked people who were experiencing psychological difficulties to undertake a kindness intervention?

Here's a statement that may or may not apply to you: *I am nervous about mixing with people I don't know well.* In a study conducted at the University of British Columbia in Canada, students were asked if this sort of statement applied to them and if they said yes, they were then recruited into the research programme. It meant all the participants were people who experienced at least some degree of social anxiety. The students were then split into three groups at random.

The first group, a control group, was simply asked to keep a written list of three things that happened to them on each of two days a week for four weeks. Nothing very scary there. But the second group was asked to deliberately engage in three separate social interactions on each of two days a week for four weeks. They were given examples such as asking a stranger for the time, chatting with a neighbour or asking someone to lunch – though in the end they could do what they liked. (They were trained in deep breathing exercises to help them feel more relaxed as they ventured so far outside their comfort zone.) As for the third group, I'm sure you'll have anticipated that their task was to carry out kind acts – and you've guessed it, they were to do so three times on each of two days a week for four weeks. Again, they were free to choose exactly what they did.[16]

Which strategy would you predict worked best in reducing levels of social anxiety over the period of the study? Well, those students who forced themselves to interact with people did see a reduction in stress levels over the four weeks. It seems confronting their fears head-on had a positive effect. But so did carrying out kind acts. And there was an added benefit for the students in this group. They not only found social situations less anxiety inducing, they stopped trying to avoid as many social situations. The same happened to the group who forced themselves to socialise, but not as quickly.

So, why does kindness have this special part to play in reducing social anxiety? The reason is that many people who find it hard to socialise fear that the people they talk to will react negatively – that they won't like them or will be rude to them or will think badly of them. But if you're interacting with someone specifically with the aim of doing something kind, instead of dreading how the other person might react, you're more likely to anticipate a positive response.

Even then, if you're anything like me you might feel nervous about offering help. Here's another extract from my Kindness Diary which illustrates the point.

Friday 12.15 p.m.
Was running along a street when in the distance I saw a man and a woman heaving a double mattress out of a van. The woman in particular seemed to be struggling. I thought perhaps I should offer to help. I was wearing trainers and didn't have a bag with me, so it wouldn't be that hard. Not hard to carry the mattress, but hard to make the offer. When I got nearer the couple had

taken the mattress in through the back gate and were starting to carry it up some outdoor stairs to the first floor. But to offer to help I'd have to step into their garden behind a high fence. Was that a bit intrusive? Would they mind? Maybe they didn't want my help. I thought better of it. Then afterwards I wished I had offered.

I made this entry before I knew the results of the Kindness Test which is a shame because had I known them, I might have acted differently. In the test we asked people how they felt after receiving an act of kindness. The responses were clear. People didn't say they felt intruded upon, interrupted, or offended. Far from it. Rather, most felt grateful, happy, loved, relieved, supported or warm.

That said, the biggest barrier people cited to being kinder was the fear that their actions might be misinterpreted. Sixty-six per cent of respondents gave this response, followed by not enough time to be kind and then the use of social media (we can't say in which precise way they felt that social media was a barrier).

Clearly, what you think is a kind act might not be seen that way by the person on the receiving end, but on balance I suspect many of us are too reticent about coming forward and should take the small risk that our help will sometimes be unwelcome.

It helps, of course, to ask people if they want help. A colleague of mine who is blind once told me he didn't dare pause on the kerb close to the road, because if he did, he'd find himself being dragged across the street by a passer-by, who thought they were being kind. It wasn't that my colleague didn't sometimes welcome being helped to cross the road, but he didn't want people to jump to that conclusion without checking.

Maxing your kindness boost

I hope by now I've convinced you that acting kindly can enhance your well-being and maybe even your physical health too. But while the effect is significant, it's not huge, so in order to maximise the benefits it's important to work out the best strategies for being kind. (And incidentally, if this talk of how to get the most for yourself out of being kind is making you feel uncomfortable, indeed warping the very idea of kindness, I will respond to that in the next chapter.)

First of all, acting kindly improves well-being in all of us to some extent, irrespective of age or sex or ethnicity. And the type of intervention doesn't really matter. But there are some patterns in the research that show us what works best to boost the giver's well-being. For a start, variety matters. Carrying out a range of acts aimed at a range of different people increases well-being more. And, unsurprisingly perhaps, research shows that the more often you are kind, the better you feel. Specifically, research shows that performing nine acts of kindness a week makes more difference than three.[17]

This precise number aside, I suspect most people who are inclined to be kind already know intuitively that 'more is more' which is one of the reasons why they tend to donate to a wide range of charities, some home-based and some doing work abroad, as well as volunteering for a number of projects and generally acting in a kind way in their personal interactions. I certainly have friends who epitomise the saying 'if you want something done, ask a busy person'. They're already giving up time to charitable schemes left, right and centre, but if you put out a call for people to help with a community project, they're the first to volunteer. Now we know why: they're getting such a kick out of it!

And let me stress again: there's nothing wrong with that.

Pinky Lelani was born in India 68 years ago in the city then known as Calcutta. In the 1970s she moved to the UK, later becoming a culinary expert, as well as an advocate for the rights of older Asian women. She is also a very kind person in her daily dealings with other people.

If you happen to be in the queue behind Pinky in the supermarket she might well turn around and offer you a single wrapped chocolate. And she might do the same if you're working on reception at an office she is visiting. Pinky has decided that on certain days she will take with her five luxury chocolates which she will give away to bring a little moment of joy to the people she meets.

Now, the main reason Pinky does what she does is altruism. She's just being nice. And I don't know to what extent she keeps up with the latest psychological research on kindness. But as it happens, Pinky's 'five-a-day' chocolate giveaway is especially good for her own well-being, because influential research has shown that concentrating five acts of kindness into one day gives a person more of a boost than spreading the kind acts across a week.[18] Of course, adopting this strategy, doesn't preclude kindness on other days too – and I know that Pinky is kind in ways other than handing out chocolates (and determined to promote more kindness among leaders). Nonetheless concentrating your kindness is good for the giver.

Other things help too, such as encouragement and praise from someone else.[19] Parents are right to recognise and validate kindness in their children because the children do feel boosted and hopefully will be kind again in future. As adults we should be acknowledging each other's kindness more often. It might sound like a patronising thing to say to someone, but 'what a kind thing to do' or 'that was very kind' are phrases we should use more frequently, not least because it's kind to acknowledge kindness.

The intensity and meaningfulness of the connection we make with another person when acting kindly also seems to make a difference to the boost we feel afterwards. Perhaps not surprisingly, one early study found that helping someone search for something they'd lost increased well-being more than giving directions to a person in the street.[20] In Chapter 6 we'll be looking at heroic acts – the most exceptional forms of kindness – and it is surely safe to assume that the hero who rescues a person from danger, an action that is likely to create a strong human bond even between previous strangers, receives a considerable spike in their self-esteem for all the modesty that heroes outwardly demonstrate.

So, acting in a kind way more often, in a more concentrated way, and in a more meaningful way in terms of human contact, all increase the boost we get from our acts. But what about giving money to good causes? It's better than nothing, no doubt, but surely the positive feeling we get from a monetary donation is not going to be as strong as the one we get from, say, volunteering? In fact, when Bryant Hui and his team at the University of Hong Kong brought together all the best studies and reanalysed the data, they found that giving money to charity appeared to have a *stronger* effect on the giver's well-being than volunteering, which might seem surprising – even disappointing – given that volunteering can make us new friends and maybe allow us even to see the results of our kindness.[21] But it must be said the analysis only included a few studies on charitable donations so I'm not sure we should read too much into this finding.

We can though put more weight on other findings from this study. For instance, there was no real difference in the well-being effect between formal philanthropy through a charity or informal help, such as assisting a neighbour. However, informal kindness rather than organised volunteering tended to improve overall life satisfaction, as well as a sense of accomplishment. This may be explained by the fact that everyday kindness is more spontaneous, more heartfelt perhaps – and isn't subject to rules. There are no references to be supplied and criminal record checks to be gone through, no volunteer training and safeguarding courses. Although these are clearly necessary in many cases, the problem is that they can turn wanting to do good into something akin to work, and in the process some of the joy is sucked out of volunteering.

That said, other studies have found that for certain groups of people, people with depression for instance, the structure that comes with organised volunteering is important.[22] If you are low on motivation and confidence, you sometimes need some direction and formality to help to direct your instinct for kindness.

In the Hui study, where people did volunteer, they got greater personal satisfaction from their actions if they enjoyed direct contact with the beneficiaries. This could explain why when people volunteer for charities they often want to do 'hands-on', 'front of house' tasks rather than utilise their particular skills. This can be annoying for charities. I remember when my husband worked for a big refugee agency how frustrated he got when someone with, say, website skills nonetheless said they wanted to volunteer in the daycentre kitchen, serving food to destitute asylum seekers. 'We really need our website updated,' my husband would moan. 'Some pro bono advice from this guy would be much more helpful to the cause than him doling out soup!' Still, I can see why the web designer acted as he did. As well as doing something that wasn't just a mirror image of his day job, he got the immediate satisfaction that comes from helping someone directly in need and seeing the impact on that person.

It is perhaps obvious that there's an added boost from having contact with the person you are helping, but does it make much, if any difference if that person is a stranger or a friend?

To find out, Oliver Scott Curry (who we've already met in this chapter) and Lee Rowland at Oxford University recruited more than 600 people online from 29 different countries. They then randomly split the recruits into different groups. The first group was instructed to carry out one act of kindness a day for a week directed at someone they were close to. The next group was told to be kind to a stranger or someone they didn't know well. The third group was instructed to do something kind for themselves each day. The fourth group simply observed acts of kindness, and the fifth group, the control group, just carried on with life as usual and didn't have to do anything in particular.

The results showed that people from all groups felt happier at the end of the week, compared with the control group. More interestingly, there really wasn't much difference in the size of the boost experienced by people who were kind to friends or to strangers. Most interesting of all, the same was true of the participants who either observed kindness or were kind to themselves.[23] The lesson from this is that if you want a well-being boost it doesn't really matter who you are kind to. Anyone will do!

Another study in this area which threw up some interesting results was conducted by the social psychologist Lara Aknin. A member of Lara's team approached people as they walked across a university campus and gave them $10.[24] This giveaway was to ensure that people had some cash to spare because next they were shown an advert for a charity which funded clean water projects in Africa. In half the cases, the researcher said that they knew the charity personally, in the other cases, the researcher didn't mention such a personal connection. All the people who'd been given $10 were then asked if they'd wish to donate.

The average sum donated per person was $5 – not the most generous amount perhaps, as it meant on average participants had simply pocketed half the money they'd been given earlier. But the findings were interesting, nonetheless. First, there was *no* significant difference in the amounts given by the two groups. Hearing that the person asking for the donation had a personal connection to the charity didn't increase – or for that matter, decrease – the size of the donation. It did make a difference, though, to the sense of happiness experienced by the givers. The ones who thought they were giving to a charity connected to the person asking for a donation felt happier about it.

What charities are to make of this finding I'm not sure. In some ways it's disappointing because the most important thing for NGOs is to maximise their income. On the other hand, the study shows that generating any sense of personal connection makes the donor feel happier and maybe that can convert into a longer-term commitment to the charity. It also perhaps suggests why so-called 'chugging' (charity mugging) – in which people are paid to approach passers-by in the street, asking them to take out a direct debit to a charity – has limited returns for charities. The chuggers appear to be hired for the gig rather than being long-term employees or volunteers of the charity, which makes for a highly transactional encounter, for all the high-octane enthusiasm on display. I don't doubt that it's a tough job, but personally, I'm much more disposed to give when I'm approached by a person I know has been devoted to the charity for many years.

Incidentally, Lara Aknin also carried out a nice study in which volunteers were given a Starbucks voucher and one of four different instructions as to how to use it. Those given the first option were to go to a coffee shop on their own to spend the voucher. Maybe a venti salted caramel mocha frappucino, with five pumps of frap roast, four pumps of caramel sauce, four pumps of caramel syrup, three pumps of mocha, three pumps of toffee nut syrup, double blended with extra whipped cream (this, I'm told, is possible) or maybe something simpler. It was up to them. The second group were told to give the voucher to a friend. The third were to go with a friend to Starbucks, and to spend the voucher on coffee for themselves, while the friend presumably paid for their own. The final, fourth option was to again invite a friend, but this time to spend the vouchers on coffees for both them and the friend.[25] The results were clear: those who took the fourth option were the happiest at the end of the day. So doing a favour *and* socialising at the same time boosts human connections even more.

Overall, we still don't really know whether giving time or money makes us happiest. It's perhaps one of those 'more research is needed' questions. Or maybe it isn't. After all, the world needs both donors and volunteers, so perhaps it's best that we self-select which of these options we want to do at any particular time. In the end, any act of kindness is a good thing, for both the recipient and the bestower and there is perhaps a certain nerdiness – I plead guilty as charged – about wanting to precisely calculate which actions achieve the best results.

LAST ACT OF KINDNESS
RECEIVED

The Kindness Test

Knowing that I was struggling with my mental health, my colleague completed our shared work.

I nearly missed a train and got on at the back when my seat was at the front. The guard carried my suitcase through eight carriages.

I found my chickens had been killed by a fox or a dog. I was very upset and my neighbour came to my aid in dealing with the carnage.

Someone baked me brownies as a thank you.

A busy plumber came over at short notice to fix a leak in the house where I was cat sitting and he didn't even charge for his services.

I am a cake decorator and one of my customers took time out to write a lovely review on my Facebook page.

Knowing that I sing in a choir, a neighbour gave me a full score of Handel's Messiah *that she had found in some old papers.*

Wife returned from hospital after six months with a brain tumour and she thanked me for all the support, care and understanding shown to her.

A seagull pooped on my head and a waitress who witnessed it rushed out of a restaurant with a cloth and cleaned it off me, which was very sweet of her.

3

DON'T GET TOO HUNG UP ON MOTIVES

Abie was only 17 and still at high school in Manhattan when he read the magazine article which prompted him to carry out an extraordinary act of kindness – one that would dominate the next few years of his life. The feature concerned the number of people who were dying while they waited for a kidney transplant and he made a split-second decision: he would become a kidney donor. Not to a relative or someone he knew, but to save the life of a stranger.

Before he could act though, he had to do something else: tell his mother. He was still a minor, so he needed her permission to become a donor. But the moment never seemed quite right to have this difficult conversation and he kept putting it off. One morning he finally plucked up the courage. It was early; he and his mother were having breakfast. She was still in her pyjamas.

'There's something I want to do,' Abie said suddenly. 'I'm young and healthy and I want to donate a kidney to a stranger.'

His mother was understandably surprised and worried. Indeed, she was adamant that he mustn't do it. 'You're only 17. What's the rush? Do it later when you can be sure you won't regret it. Your brain's still developing until you're 25. It's too early to take such a big decision.'

Abie though was on the school debating team and had marshalled his arguments. He knew the statistics supported his position. The risk to him was low, while the benefit to the recipient of his kidney was high, indeed it was life-saving. So he was desperate to go ahead and eventually his mother realised that he wasn't going to be deterred.

Abie started investigating how to make his offer of a kidney, hoping he could have the operation soon. But now the ethics committee at his local hospital stood in his way. Because he was so young, they insisted that he wait a year, and come back if he still wanted to do it.

You'll have worked out by now that Abie was a very determined person. He wasn't put off. The year passed and nothing had changed his mind.

The day of the surgery dawned and the operation all went smoothly. When he came round from the anaesthetic, pumped full of painkillers, Abie felt great. But gradually the pain kicked in. It was worth it, though, because he'd been told that minutes after his kidney had been removed, it had been transplanted into the body of a young man, just a year or two older than him. A stranger.

This young man, whose life had been saved by Abie, was also recovering in the same hospital. Abie was soon up and about, at first gingerly, then more confidently. The same was true of the recipient of his kidney. In other circumstances, their paths might have crossed as they walked the hospital corridors. There were no ethical reasons preventing them from meeting, but they were deliberately kept apart. This was because they'd agreed to meet each other for the first time on live TV, an experience which Abie says he found much more scary than donating a kidney and one that makes for a riveting and very moving watch. I've put a link to the video in the notes at the end of this book.[1]

Now Abie is the first to admit that he had something to gain from his supposedly selfless act. He loved that he had helped someone else in such a transformative way. But does that mean his kindness wasn't pure, that it was contaminated? Abie answered the question this way when I interviewed him for a BBC radio series on kindness.

> 'It's not completely pure because I enjoyed it so much. It was adventurous, it was fun. I derive pleasure from living in accordance with my values and I get to text the person who got my kidney and get updates on his life. It certainly doesn't feel very self-sacrificial.'[2]

I've told you the story of Abie at some length because the question of 'purity' often arises when kindness is discussed. For example, having read the previous chapter, you now know that acting kindly might improve your well-being. Are you compromised as a result? Is any future act of kindness you perform going to be undermined in some way? Will your act of kindness have less impact on the recipient and indeed on you?

For some experts, motivation matters so much that they argue a kind act can almost become *un*kind if the motives are not purely altruistic and selfless. Others have a more relaxed view and take an 'ends justifying the means' approach. But either way, there is no doubt that motives complicate kindness in all sorts of ways, and that can make people doubt whether they've actually done a good thing or not.

To illustrate the point cast your mind back to Season 5, Episode 4 of the TV show *Friends*. It's called 'The One Where Phoebe Hates PBS', but could just as easily be called 'The One About Whether There's Any Such Thing as a Selfless Good Deed'.

The storyline revolves around Joey saying he's doing good by taking part in a charity telethon on PBS (the Public Broadcasting Service in the US). Phoebe disputes his claim, saying he mainly wants to get on television. He hits back saying it was the same when she acted as a surrogate mother to her brother's triplets. Yes, it was a really kind thing to do, but it made her feel good about herself, so that makes it selfish. In fact, Joey declares – he's really fired up now – there's no such thing as an unselfish good deed.

Phoebe vows to prove him wrong, only to discover that she has set herself an oddly difficult task. Her first kind act involves raking up the leaves for an old man who lives nearby. This is truly selfless, right? Well, no because the old man comes out with cider and cookies, and she can't help feeling she's done a wonderful thing. Next, she lets a bee sting her in the park. Huh? (Remember, this is Phoebe logic we're dealing with here.) It's a good deed, she argues, because there's nothing in it for her, while the bee gets to look tough in front of his friends. But Joey points out that the bee probably died in the process – so how kind was that? In the end, Phoebe makes a pledge of $200 to the PBS telethon, even though she doesn't want to give such a large sum away and had been planning to use the money to buy a hamster. But this too backfires, because her donation, made through

Joey who is volunteering on the phone bank, pushes the combined pledges over last year's record. Joey gets interviewed by the host and so has his moment of TV stardom after all. This makes Phoebe feel she's helped her friend and leaves her feeling good about herself again. It seems that Joey is right after all.

Now, sorry if I've spoiled the plot for an episode of *Friends* you've not seen yet (though is there anyone left in the world who hasn't seen every minute of *Friends?*), but you get the point. A kind act can often have an upside for us, whether we like it or not – as Phoebe discovered. But to what extent does this fact devalue the kind act? At this point, I nail my colours to the mast and say that I don't think the kindness is devalued. If your action is well meant and genuinely benefits the recipient, the fact that you know it will give you a boost as well doesn't diminish the action's intrinsic good. But that of course is a point of view and I always like to have some evidence to back up any contention, so let's turn to the science.

Mixed motivations

Let's begin with evolution. One of the most obvious and frequent forms of kindness is the kindness we show towards our own children and other relatives. This is known as kin altruism and is fundamental to the success of humankind. And yet it's not 'pure' altruism in the sense that only the receiver benefits. We have sex so that our species will survive after we're dead – put like that, it's a selfless act. But let's face it, sex is also fun. We've evolved so that our bodies and brains give us intense pleasure in the act of procreation. Likewise, labour, childbirth and child rearing involve a lot of self-sacrifice – much of it by the mother – and at the biological level we put up with the pain and effort because we want our genes to survive in the form of this new human being and so be passed on. But, more than that, we gain personal joy and fulfilment from nurturing offspring. And yet, coming full circle, we don't give up many of the best years of our life to bring up children just because it gives us pleasure. The motivations for having a family and looking after our relatives are mixed up together – part selfish, part selfless.

More overtly, we all practise what is known as reciprocal altruism where we do a favour in the hope that the favour might be returned at a later date.[3] For example, I make an effort to be friendly and welcoming to people who move into our street in south London. I act this way partly because I'm a good person, I hope, partly because it makes me feel good, and partly because I hope my new neighbour will be nice and supportive in their turn. I put out their recycling bins and water their garden when they are on holiday; they do the same for me when I'm away. In his blog the Dalai Lama jokes that if you really want to be selfish you should be altruistic, because if you help everyone else, when you really need help they'll help you too. But he makes a more serious point in the same blog about the time in your life when things go wrong or your health fails.

'That is the moment when we learn who is really helpful and who is completely useless. So to prepare for that moment, to make genuine friends who will help us when the need arises, we ourselves must cultivate altruism!'[4]

Acting kindly can have another benefit too, especially if it's public, for it can make us look good, improve our reputation with others, and enhance our sense of self-worth. Indeed, sometimes people take this to another level in what's known as competitive altruism.[5] Anyone who's been to a charity auction will have watched as two people (usually men in my experience, either because they like the competition or have more money – who knows?) compete to pay way over the odds for a week in a villa in Italy or a dinner at a fancy restaurant. This willy waggling (please excuse the technical term) can be pretty nauseating for people watching on, but the participants seem to think it makes them look good and, hey ho, in the end, the good cause gains from this behaviour, so is it really such a problem? As one very experienced fundraiser, Lyndall Stein said to me, although charities have ethical policies governing which types of companies they will take money from, when it comes to individuals they tend to be more relaxed.

'It's money and we need the money. You can't actually interrogate every single person's motive for giving because if you go down that route you just end up having nothing. Some people might give because they are truly empathic and noble. Some people like giving because they want to show off to their friends at an auction. But does that contaminate the money? No, I don't think so, because the needs are great.'[6]

When the evolutionary biologist Nichola Raihani analysed the online sponsorship forms for more than 2,500 people entering the London Marathon in 2014, she found a striking pattern. On fundraising sites, you can of course see how much the people before you have donated and when one donor gives a much larger than average amount, subsequent donors do tend to give a bit more too. What Raihani found though was that when a man gave a large donation to a marathon runner who was rated by many as an attractive woman, the subsequent men, not to be outdone, gave almost four times the average amount.[7] Such generosity is to be welcomed of course, and I doubt that the women marathon runners minded one bit, but clearly the actions of these men weren't purely philanthropic. No, they were showing off, strutting their stuff, flashing the cash, even flirting maybe.

But this isn't the whole picture. For about one in eight people making a donation chooses to be anonymous on fundraising sites, so not everyone is trying to take the opportunity to big themselves up. Reassuringly, Nichola Raihani – who as a result of her analysis might have good grounds for regarding much online giving as cynically motivated – told me that she still believes in pure kindness, though now we're back with the issue of whether the term 'pure kindness' is really meaningful at all. As I've said, I incline to the view that most if not all acts of kindness are born of mixed motives. I've already discussed volunteering. I know a number of people who have helped to cook and serve turkey and all the trimmings to the homeless on Christmas Day. Clearly, these friends are doing a very kind thing, but all admit that they partly do it because it is fun, it's a different way of spending Christmas, they get to meet a lot of nice people and, yes, they can tell people about it afterwards!

When we choose to behave kindly, we shouldn't worry if our motivations are mixed. Advocates for kindness might do well to throw out the very concept of pure kindness – or even 'grading' levels of kindness according to some scale of selflessness – and instead argue that any extrinsically kind act 'counts' as kindness, irrespective of its motivation. For the longer our list of different motivations for acting in a kind way, the more likely we are to act – and that's what matters.

Finally, let's turn to neuroscience to see what it can tell us about the purity or not of our intentions when we perform certain kind acts – and indeed, whether this matters or not. Be warned, this is quite a complicated line of argument.

The study I'm drawing on was carried out by neuroscientists Dan Campbell-Meiklejohn and Jo Cutler at Sussex University. They combined and reanalysed data from the brain scans of more than a thousand people from a range of different studies. In some of these experiments, people lying in brain scanners played various well-known games of trust and cooperation, such as the prisoner's dilemma and the dictator game, games played on a computer where you get to decide how generous or mean you want to be to your opponent. In other studies, participants were given money and then asked if they would like to donate some of it to charity. Sometimes the choices people were asked to make were purely altruistic – they were acts of selfless generosity with no opportunity for personal gain. At other times, the generous acts could also benefit the person taking the action. They were partly strategic. So, for example, behaving generously could result in a player doing better in the game further down the line.

What Cutler and Campbell-Meiklejohn found when they looked at all these studies was that several established areas of the reward system in the brain were activated regardless of whether the acts were more purely altruistic or partly altruistic/partly strategic. But there were differences too. What the pair discovered are in effect the distinct neural signatures of these two types of kind act. So, when people were making purely altruistic decisions there was more activity in several areas including the subgenual area of the anterior cingulate cortex, but when participants made strategic decisions, involving both altruism and an element of self-interest, there was more activity in several different areas, including the nucleus accumbens.

Which is all very interesting, perhaps, but so what? What, if anything, is this information telling us? Well, first of all, both of these areas of the brain become active when we encounter something pleasurable. But the fact that there is a difference is interesting. The neuroscientists seem to have found a distinction between the 'warm glow' of pure altruism and the pleasure of a different kind of altruism where you also have something to gain yourself. And where it gets really interesting is that it can even be argued that this latter response in the brain is stronger, perhaps because it combines the joy of altruism plus the joy of whatever you stood to gain.

Perhaps the most important finding is that the brain is primed to reward kindness *whatever* the intention behind it, using different combinations of parts of the brain to do so, but doing so nonetheless. And of course, there's a feedback loop operating here. We initiate a kind act – 'go on, help that old lady across the road' – then register the act – 'duly noted' – and finally applaud it – 'well done, doesn't that feel good?'. In a sense, whatever the motivation for acting kindly in the first place, subsequent acts of kindness in part stem from the fact that your brain makes you feel good about acting in this way.

In addition, there might also be a neuroscientific explanation for extraordinary acts of altruism, like Abie giving his kidney to a stranger. This comes from the work of the neuroscientist Abigail Marsh who scanned the brains of extraordinary altruists like Abie. In her research, she was interested not in which parts of the brain become active, like in the studies on strategic altruism that I was discussing above, but in the size and shape of different parts of the brain which vary between different people.

Of particular interest to her was the amygdala, a walnut-shaped area deep inside the brain which is considered to be the seat of some (but not all) emotions, one of them being fear. And when Marsh measured the size of this area in kidney donors, fittingly she discovered something extraordinary about these extraordinary altruists: their amygdalae were on average 8% larger than other (less altruistic or ordinary) people's.[8]

This was striking, because as well as processing our own fear, the amygdala is also important for us in being able to understand how other people feel and therefore to empathise with them. And what Professor Marsh concluded was that extraordinary altruists with their bigger amygdalae are likely to be better at imagining what it's like to know that you have kidney failure and that your life is at risk, while the rest of us, with our average-sized amygdalae, will find that harder.

Moreover, when she put people with psychopathic tendencies into the scanner their amygdalae were smaller than average.[9] This follows because psychopaths aren't concerned about other people's feelings at all. They don't tend to feel afraid themselves and so they don't empathise with the fear of others.

All of this leads Marsh to posit the idea of a continuum of kindness, with the psychopaths at one end, the extraordinary altruists at the other end and the rest of us spread out in between.

Then there is the big question of whether people are born with these brain differences. Because if they are, rather than being exceptionally kind people through their own efforts, the extraordinary altruists might simply be 'programmed' from birth to be kind due to their large amygdalae.

This, it turns out, is part but not all of the story. Yes, the size of your amygdalae in adulthood is partly inherited, but it's also based on the experiences you have growing up. So, people who suffer extreme deprivation and neglect might have amygdalae that develop more slowly and end up smaller than they would otherwise have been, while those brought up in warm, loving homes, could end up with a larger than inherited amygdala size.[10]

This means that extraordinary altruists are partly born and partly made (as a result of their upbringing and environment) – but on top of that, that they can become more extraordinary still through a process of positive feedback. So, thanks to their large and (sometimes) growing amygdalae they are better at understanding how others feel and this prompts them to act kindly. But also, each act of kindness they perform reinforces the sense of self-worth they feel which in turn can lead them to be kinder and kinder. They are, in other words, benefitting from a sort of kindness ratchet. Which is great for them. But what about the rest of us?

Well, if there is a continuum, we too should be able to move up the scale, towards the extraordinary altruists. But, of course, there's also the possibility that we could move down, towards the psychopaths. And while the size of our amygdalae will have some bearing on where we are on the continuum, we still retain a lot of agency in the process. Nature, nurture and good practice all come into the equation.

To sum up, there's no reason to try to grade levels of kindness according to how much the person acting kindly gives and gains from their action. The fact is that all acts of kindness involve some sacrifice, but also some benefit. In real life, kindness is almost always win/win, and not zero-sum, which is why there is so much to be gained from trying to increase the stock of kindness in the world.

Overdoing kindness

So far in this book, I've been suggesting that committing yourself to being kind to others and looking out for every opportunity to do kind acts is a good thing – and always welcomed. On the whole, I hold to that position and I suspect you do too. But of course, an act of kindness can simply backfire, causing more harm than good.

When I was at junior school my grandparents gave me a bag from Jersey Zoo, a very seventies bag, which would look cool in a retro way these days. I already had a similar bag however, so although I was old enough to know that I needed to thank my grandparents enthusiastically, I later gave the bag to a friend of mine at school. But she was worried her mother might think she had stolen it – her mother was quite strict – so I remember us kneeling down on the break-your-arm concrete of the playground so that I could write with pencil on a scrap of paper that this was a present for my friend because I didn't need the bag. A sweet thing to do? You might think so, but no. The next day my friend brought the bag back and told me her mother was furious with her for accepting it.

At the time I was puzzled, and my friend was very upset. She wanted the bag and didn't understand why she couldn't have it. Now, of course, I see why my friend's mother felt uncomfortable. The family were struggling financially and she didn't appreciate being shown up by an act of charity from a seven-year-old, however well meaning. Indeed, my story chimes with a common scene in TV dramas and films when one character's offer of help is rejected with a heartfelt cry of, 'I don't *want* your charity'.

Research shows that offers of assistance that induce feelings of helplessness or leave people feeling indebted and obliged to return the favour are often not received well.[11] It is something we should all consider carefully when trying to be kind to people, particularly if we don't know them well or don't know the full consequences of our giving.

Another problem that some have with kindness, particularly in this age of social media, is that it can seem showy and self-aggrandising. The term 'virtue signalling' has been invented to call out this sort of behaviour. For example, the charitable actions of the rock star Bono, or the film star Emma Thompson, seem to incite irritation, rather than admiration in some. 'There they are on their fancy yachts or in their Hampstead homes, showing off about how much they care about Amazonian tribes or refugees. It's all about making them look good – and they can easily afford it.'

Personally I'm not sure it's fair to chide the charitable and kindly actions of Bono and Emma Thompson in this way, when those actions not only benefit people, but bring the charity publicity they wouldn't get if they were only to help in private. But for those who disapprove, this would be an example of what's technically called 'tainted altruism'. This can be a particular issue when kindness is shown to strangers. Such kindness doesn't feel quite natural to some people, perhaps out of the instinct that you look after your own and charity begins at home.

For example, those who donate kidneys to family members are rarely questioned, but people like Abie who give kidneys to people they don't know sometimes find that their motives are impugned. Perhaps this is because we wouldn't do it ourselves and so we think these apparently kindly souls are only becoming donors to show off about how virtuous they are. As the US-based professor of philanthropy, Sara Konrath, said to me when I interviewed her on this subject, maybe it suits some people to believe there's no such thing as pure kindness and to question people's motives, because this gives them an excuse *not* to carry out kind actions themselves. When other people are a lot kinder than us, we can feel defensive and feel the need to explain why we don't do the same. If Abie can give away his kidney, why can't the rest of us? It's makes us uneasy. So sometimes it's easier to criticise a person's motives, to make us feel a bit better about our own decisions.

But maybe there really are some people who are kind just to get attention? In other words, is it *all* about the attention and nothing to do with helping others? Sara Konrath set out to find out, with experiments targeting people who are narcissistic, who love showing off and who have low levels of empathy for other people.

Remember the ice bucket challenge back in 2014? The idea was to film yourself having a bucket of iced water poured over your head, post it online and then challenge someone else to do the same. It was all to raise awareness and funding for amyotrophic lateral sclerosis, the most common type of motor neurone disease. In some versions of the game the rule was that if you didn't want to have icy water dumped on you then you had to make a donation to the charity. In others, if you did the ice bucket challenge you still made a small donation, but if you didn't you had to make a much larger one. It was up to you. The idea went viral with more than 17 million videos posted on Facebook.

Professor Konrath recruited 9,000 people to fill in an online survey, asking them whether they'd heard of the ice bucket challenge, had done it, had challenged someone else to do it, had donated money and/or had posted a video of it. At the same time, the respondents were also asked to answer questions assessing their narcissistic tendencies. As she expected, Professor Konrath found that a high number of narcissists were drawn to this very public way of doing good.[12] But – here's the killer finding – while this group were more likely than other people to post a video, they mainly did so without making a donation to the charity. Now to be fair in some versions of the challenge this is allowed. But even so, no one was stopping those who did the challenge from donating money as well and in contrast to the narcissists, people who scored lower on narcissism tended only to give (the less showy option) and people in between both gave money and had icy water poured over their heads (so were generous *and* good sports).

Before we dismiss narcissists altogether, I should cite a

further study of this group. This one looked at their propensity to volunteer and the good news (for them and us) is that they were no less (though also no more) likely to volunteer than less self-centred people. However – and no surprise here – they were more likely to carry out public rather than private acts of kindness. It was still partly about showing off, then. Also, when it came to the motive for helping others, people who scored high on empathy set more store on the importance of altruism than the narcissists did. This led Konrath to wonder whether this means that narcissists are also less likely to experience the warm glow of giving. If there was any justice in the world, this would be true, but as yet there's no evidence to confirm Konrath's speculation.

Finally, in this section, as well as narcissistic kindness and tainted altruism, there is perhaps such a thing as ill-directed kindness or kindness overloads.

Take the example of Pete, a 90-year-old widower who every day was going to his local pub in Chelmsford for a glass of red wine and plate of Hunter's chicken. The landlord of the pub was very taken by this charming old gentleman, who he suspected was lonely, and this led him to post Pete's story on social media. The post went viral and the upshot was that masses of people rang up the pub and paid in advance for Pete's wine and lunch. If you watch the video on Twitter you'll see Pete's reaction when he hears that his next 90 glasses of wine have already been paid for.[13] It's a lovely moment.

Now, you'd have to have a heart of stone not to find this incident heartwarming, and there is absolutely nothing wrong, quite the contrary, with people buying a lonely old man his lunch and a glass of wine. But at the same time, there are clearly tens of millions of people around the world who are in greater need. The problem is that we don't know these people, while through the power of social media we do know Pete (or at least we think we do). By showing kindness to him and not to others we are indulging in what psychology terms 'the identifiable victim effect'.[14] Charities know all about this effect which is why they often front their fundraising appeals with a single 'case study', focusing on one survivor, rather than bombarding potential donors with overwhelming numbers.

I have an example in front of me as I write; one of those leaflets that fall out of the Sunday paper. It is for the charity Sightsavers and features a tiny little crying girl, with the appeal: 'Nalukena gets closer to blindness with every blink. Just £5 could save her sight.' As a presenter of a BBC World Service programme on global health I know that hundreds of thousands of children, and indeed adults, suffer blindness for want of simple, cheap treatments and that information should be enough to spur me to give to charities like Sightsavers. But it is the sight of little Nalukena that really gets to me. I know I'm not alone.

In an ideal world we wouldn't need to be emotionally manipulated in this way, but the fact is we do find it much easier to empathise with a named individual than with an anonymous group. For example, in the Kindness Test when people were asked which types of charities they donate money to, causes at home were more popular than causes abroad, which is of course completely up to them. And if you slide people into a brain scanner and show them photos of actual people in need, their brain shows a pattern of response that reveals that at a neurological level we have more empathy towards people who we see as like us.[15]

The brutal fact is that we are drawn to people who are similar to us. For instance, as we'll see in more detail in Chapter 5, we even like people better if they have the same birthday as us, despite knowing full well that this is the most random of connections. We constantly look for what we have in common and when we establish a link, we find it easier to act in a kindly way towards people, or at least not show indifference.

We should – and with effort can – fight this instinct and try to direct kindness more widely and – in the broadest sense – more fairly. At the same time, any act of kindness is better than none, so if you want to buy Pete's 91st glass of wine, don't let me stop you. Feeling good about yourself as you watch Pete looking so happy is fine too. As is turning over the page on the Sightsavers leaflet and seeing the 'after' photo of Nalukena, beaming joyfully now that she's receiving an antibiotic which has cured her trachoma.

Consider your own self-interest

To conclude this chapter, having examined the evidence carefully, and at the risk of repeating myself once too often, I don't believe that the fact that acting in a kind way makes us feel good, in any serious way negates the benefit of that kindness to others. Indeed, I'd go further and say that there isn't really such a thing as entirely selfless kindness and that this is a good thing. Kindness doesn't have to mean acting like a saint at all times, but rather being a decent, cooperative human being, who sometimes gains as well as gives through their actions.

The community organising charity Citizens UK teaches its leaders and volunteers to always consider their self-interest when planning community actions. They argue that taking into account what you get out of an action strengthens that action and improves the chances of it succeeding.[16]

So, for example, you might be asked to join a volunteer team of neighbours in creating a community garden at the end of your street in order to give local people with no outside space a chance to grow things and a place to sit on warm evenings. If you live in a flat with no balcony your motivation for joining the team is partly altruistic, partly self-interested, as you will directly benefit, along with others. Meanwhile, if you do have a garden of your own, your motivation may be that the community garden will make the street look nicer, perhaps even increase house prices. Either way, you have personally gained from the action, increasing the motivation to take part, but surely not diminishing the fact that you have acted in a communitarian way – giving up your time for a project that brings joy to others.

Of course, the commitment of time and effort, partly to help others, might be viewed as a real cost. But this surely misses the key point. Because even this cost brings some benefit to the giver, whether it be the joy of taking part in a shared enterprise or the fitness gain from lugging and digging and planting.

I have seen an example of this in a scheme to support refugees to which I am connected personally in a small way. The scheme is called Community Sponsorship and it was introduced in the UK in 2016, adapted from a model that has been running successfully in Canada since the late 1970s. It allows local people to come together to settle one refugee family in their neighbourhood. The group has to secure a house for that family and then be approved by the Home Office. If approval is granted, the group then picks up the family from the airport, provides them with a warm welcome to the community and assists them in setting up things like bank accounts and GP surgery registrations and school places for their children. The volunteers then help the family members to learn English, attend training courses and find work.

Where I live in south-east London, Peckham Sponsors Refugees was formed back in 2018, with the aim of welcoming one refugee family from Syria. Because I am so busy – I really am – I wasn't a key member of this group myself, but I saw the efforts of others – including a number of friends and neighbours – and so was motivated to help when and where I could.

I particularly remember a weekend after the group had secured a house that the refugee family – then in Jordan – could rent when they got to Britain. The house was owned by a very kind and generous Italian woman, who had agreed to drop the rent substantially below the market rate so that it would be affordable for the family when they arrived. It was a nice house in a pleasant area, but needed some refurbishment to make it a welcoming home. This is when I got involved.

The day I spent with other volunteers cleaning, sponge and paint roller in hand, was a truly happy and fulfilling experience. Yes, I suppose it was kind of me to give up a day to decorate a house for refugees I hadn't at that point met, but it was hardly a great sacrifice of time on my part and the warm feeling I got from doing it represented considerable payback.

The efforts of Peckham Sponsors Refugees were picked up in local media and around the country – as was true with many other groups – and not least because sponsorship volunteers seemed to have such fun being involved, other people were motivated to start groups. Now there are hundreds of groups around the country, with more springing up all the time.

It all shows that there are so many positive effects that stem from acting in a kind way. Of course, at root, sponsoring a refugee family to come to your community is an act of sheer altruism. The main beneficiaries are the refugees themselves, who get to build a new life in safety and security, with a network of locals looking out for them. But every community sponsorship volunteer I've met – and I've now met a lot – say they got more out of the experience than they put in. Meanwhile, their example leads directly to others being kind in the same way – that is, setting up a community sponsorship group of their own or maybe joining a different kind of project. And then kindness begets kindness with the settled refugees themselves often getting involved in local efforts to help others.

LAST KIND ACT CARRIED OUT
FOR SOMEONE ELSE

The Kindness Test

I met a hot, tired person walking in opposite direction. He was going to a pub. I phoned the pub and paid for a pint for him when he arrived.

I didn't turn on the coffee grinder while my father listened to a radio programme.

I started a conversation with a stranger.

I found out the Courtauld Gallery was reopening and sent the information about it to my mother, with whom I had been studying the Impressionists.

A newly promoted person at work is making mistakes. I gave them reassurance about the things they're getting right.

I told my wife I loved her.

I allowed a pregnant woman to use the pub toilet before me.

I was working in an A&E department as a volunteer and sat with someone who was very upset.

Rolled a cigarette for a stranger who asked.

I was playing bridge and I didn't double as it would have made our opponents despondent.

SOCIAL MEDIA IS FULL OF KINDNESS (OK, NOT FULL, BUT IT IS THERE)

At the reception after a friend's wedding earlier this year I was seated next to an MP. She was friendly, open and modest – a person you could imagine people liking, regardless of their politics. In her face-to-face dealings my guess is that most people treat her politely and respect her position as an elected representative. But when it comes to social media, it's a different story.

She is, she told me, subject to the vilest, violent threats on a daily basis. This, sadly, is a fairly common story these days. MPs, particularly female MPs – and among them, particularly women of colour – tend to report that they are regularly targeted on social media. I remember another MP saying she has stopped wearing an Apple watch as she risked seeing another death threat whenever she glanced at the time.

This hatred is directed at other prominent people too. And less high-profile people don't escape. Almost anyone who uses social media platforms can suffer online abuse, with a whole lexicon of new terms now capturing this: there's trolling, flaming, doxing and pile-ons.

It didn't surprise any of us on the team behind the Kindness Test that social media was identified as one of the places where kindness was seen least frequently, and there is no doubt that some of the content on these platforms can be deeply unpleasant, presenting the most dismal view of humanity. But as with other areas of life, there is a danger that we can become fixated on the negative, while down-playing the positive. In fact, many of the posts and exchanges on social media show the kinder side of human nature. And we have it in our power to make social media an even kinder place, if we avoid posting angry and hateful material ourselves, stop liking and reposting such material posted by others and engage with more thoughtful material instead.

Before we despair, we need to remember that the views we see online are almost certainly not an accurate reflection of all the views out there. For a start, being online is a bit like driving – just as we sit in the anonymous bubble of our cars and vent our fury at other motorists, in the echo chambers online we seem to feel safe revealing the angry side of our characters. Also, there is plenty of evidence that posts expressing moral outrage online get more attention; they're more frequently liked and shared. And that's where the problem starts.

Using machine learning software, a team at Yale University tracked moral outrage in real time in Twitter posts. Twelve million tweets later they had demonstrated that over time, the more our angry tweets are liked, the angrier we make our subsequent tweets.[1] We are perversely incentivised to move away from giving thoughtful, measured responses and towards sharing views that are ever more extreme.

You can experience for yourself how big a following you

get if you say outrageous things by having a go at a game called Bad News, devised by the Cambridge University social psychologist Sander van der Linden. You play online using a (thankfully) fake social media site, where you choose what to post from various options and then watch to see how many extra followers each post gets you.[2] The more extreme your posts, the more your number of followers rockets. The game illustrates the kinds of tactics that some people are deliberately employing on social media in order to entice you into helping them to spread misinformation – tactics such as fearmongering, inventing fake experts and promoting conspiracy theories.

Now you might think van der Linden's experiment would have the harmful effect of encouraging unkindness online because it shows that bad stuff works if you want a large following. But in fact, his aim is the opposite. He wants to lift the lid on how it all works, so that we know when we're being manipulated. People who played his games were better afterwards at spotting fake news headlines and said they would become more circumspect about what they shared in the future.[3]

This suggests that there are ways to counteract the malign forces that encourage people to be more and more horrible on social media. But there's obviously a long way to go, and anyway, didn't I promise at the outset that there's plenty of kindness online already? This is where I come to the defence of social media and put it to you, that it's not all bad. In fact, a lot of it is very good. It's just a question of seeing and appreciating and fostering it.

Everyday kindness online

Before social media, the only ways to wish a friend or colleague 'Happy Birthday' were to send them a birthday card or take the time to call them. Now, thanks to new tech, it is quick and easy to send greetings as a simple message, as an e-card or a birthday GIF. The result: more best wishes on the big day.

Does this expand the pool of kindness? In some cases, all that is happening is that a kindness that used to be 3D is now 2D. The actual and personal has been replaced by the virtual. The ease of using social media has certainly widened the pool of kindness, but you could argue that it's pretty shallow – more like a municipal paddling pool than a deep lake. You could also argue that if 'it's the thought that counts', the planning and effort that go into buying, writing and physically posting a birthday card are much higher than are needed to quickly type 'Happy Birthday' on your phone. In this sense, much of the kindness shown on social media has the same relation to real-world kindness as so-called 'click-tivism' does to traditional activism.

But that doesn't mean that this kindness isn't appreciated, or that it should be dismissed. If it's true that negative reactions to what we post cause real pain – and there's strong evidence that it does – so it's also true that positive reactions online evoke real pleasure. As a small example, when I posted the cover of this very book on Instagram for the first time, a good six months before the book was published, more than 400 people liked it and 20 people wrote nice comments. OK, it didn't take a lot of effort on their part for them to be nice in this way. It wasn't as if they'd gone to the trouble of writing a letter or calling me, but I still really appreciated their warm words and encouragement. More than that, without social media there wouldn't have been a way for a wide circle of people to show kindness about my forthcoming book. In this sense, then, the existence of social media has increased the total sum of human kindness, simply by providing a way to make it easier to send kind messages or positive vibes.

The most obvious kindness online is found in forums and support groups, where strangers show they care by posting positive and supportive messages to people who are sick, or trying to get pregnant or struggling with phobias. Posting on these sites is again quick and easy and some of the messages might seem banal and sentimental. But they are still heartfelt and they are still sincere. Hundreds of thousands of people are getting support in this way, support that otherwise would not be available. But that's just the tip of the iceberg.

There are also hundreds, even thousands, of sites high-lighting kind acts or giving people the opportunity to reach out and thank those who've helped them in some way. For example, on the site thankandpraise.com you can leave a message for a nurse or a teacher who was kind to you or gave you special care, and the organisation will track down the kind person and pass on your thanks. It's a lovely idea. It's a simple idea. And it only works thanks to today's technology.

We're now able, through social media, to perform many acts of micro-kindness to friends and strangers, close to home and across continents, that in aggregate can become massive shows of solidarity and compassion. As I write, the

Russian invasion of Ukraine is underway. Practical support of all kinds is being offered to Ukrainians, but there is also a surge in virtual support, an outpouring of sympathy (and yes, outrage) online. In the past it would have been much harder for citizens caught up in a war to know that people across the world were thinking of them. Nor would they have known that their plight was dominating the news abroad. And it's not as if adding a background of the Ukrainian flag to our social media profiles prevents us from making donations or offering direct help to refugees as well. Indeed, it could even increase the likelihood that we take action, as we see others expressing their empathy.

Another way in which social media has helped us to be more kind is through messaging apps such as WhatsApp. Neighbourhood or street mutual aid groups came into their own during the pandemic, allowing people to offer and request help or advice. If my street WhatsApp is anything to go by, the amount of goodness in people that can be surfaced through a quick message is extraordinary. The moment a neighbour said they'd tested positive for Covid, for example, neighbours would spring forward with offers to drop off anything they needed.

More recently, I put out an appeal on our group to see if anyone had a pram they could donate to an Afghan refugee who was due to give birth. (I'd heard about this mother's situation through another WhatsApp group I'm in.) Within five minutes, one neighbour had offered a pram that needed cleaning and mending, another immediately said they would fix it and a third offered a steam cleaner.

Again, good neighbourliness existed long before WhatsApp groups, and there is no substitute for in-person interactions to create a sense of local community in which people look out for each other. But plenty of people have made friends online and the connections made through tech can grease the wheels of neighbourhood compassion, helping to enhance social bonds and providing another outlet through which they can be strengthened. And they can evolve over time from groups where people are helping in an emergency, to platforms for grassroots campaigns or places where information (anyone know a good plumber?) is exchanged.

A cottage industry of kindness

On the first Saturday of the second lockdown in England, back in November 2020, I went out food shopping in a local market and bumped into a friend and colleague who at the time was seconded to help with top-level planning for the pandemic. He is usually quite bright and bubbly, but that day he seemed weighed down with stress and worry. He had just seen projections on the spread of the virus and was in despair, realising what a long haul the pandemic was going to be and that soon things would be moving in the wrong direction infection-wise. His gloom spread to me as we contemplated the possibility of months of lockdown ahead, which was exactly what happened, of course.

To lift our spirits, we shifted the conversation to other things. That day happened to be the day that Joe Biden was finally confirmed as the new US president after days of tension while Donald Trump persisted in claiming victory. It was not obviously a subject of light relief, but my friend's face suddenly lit up as he said that the one bright point in his day in recent weeks was turning on his phone and seeing all the funny memes that had been posted on the US presidential election.

One he – and subsequently I – really loved was a video that depicted Joe Biden playing the bongos and singing a Finnish song, sung by a Turkish singer, while Donald Trump jigs around and claps his hands joyfully. Bizarrely, a large cat looms into the side of the screen, nodding its head along to the rhythm. It's known as the vibing cat and there are different versions of course, but the Trump/Biden one is the best. If you haven't seen it, I urge you to take a look. It won't be hard to find. I don't know whether someone gained commercially from making this – or hoped to – but whatever their motives, the maker of this piece of nonsense undoubtedly spread a lot of happiness around the world. One of the comments on YouTube is from Kimberley, who says that a few days before her brother died he told her this was his favourite single video 'ever made in history' and that she is going to watch it every day.[4]

What is particularly delightful about this video is that it punctures the seriousness and bitterness of the US presidential election. It pokes fun at Trump in particular, but not in a vicious way. It just makes him – and to be fair, Biden – seem bumbling and ludicrous. When I saw it, I was genuinely fearful about where America was heading – this video was some welcome light relief.

Or earlier in the pandemic, maybe you were one of the hundreds of thousands of people to watch videos online of the BBC commentator, Andrew Cotter, who, with no real sports events to commentate on, commentated on the activities of his labradors Olive and Mabel as they 'competed' in

'The Dog's Breakfast Grand Final' and to see which of them could be more naughty on a walk in the woods. He was entertaining himself, but the videos were soon spreading joy across Britain and around the world during a very difficult time for everyone.

You'll have your own example of a GIF or meme or joke or whatever that lightened your day, which made you laugh. I like a little-known dog on Instagram @herbertdoggins. He is a terrier who belongs to a colleague called Victoria. She seems to have captured his 'voice' perfectly. 'Magnificent Hair Day!' he'll say as his mane blows wildly in the wind. Herbert has 154 followers, so he's not some huge social media sensation, but I smile when I see him. Whether it's pandas going on slides or babies laughing as paper is torn up in front of them, there are of course mountains of this stuff all over social media – and each act of creation and sharing, while also being acts of self-promotion to an extent, are surely also little acts of kindness.

How we can actively make social media kinder

But what about the hate? Hopefully the law and regulation will eventually find better ways of dealing with the criminal threats, the harassment and the misinformation. Meanwhile there is also something we can do about some of the anger, the negativity and criticism on social media. We can choose to like the kind comments and ignore the unkind. We can follow people who post positive things and unfollow anyone who's mean. Engagement matters too and we don't have to engage. We can amplify the good and isolate the bad. The haters and ranters on social media are like toddlers behaving badly – they want your attention. Don't give it to them.

Then there is the problem of so-called 'doom-scrolling', where you can't resist looking at the latest updates on the pandemic/Ukraine/climate change/insert-the-current-distressing-story-in-the-news-here and end up absorbing nothing but negative news. Unless you avoid the news and social media altogether (which might have other conse-quences) you are going to be confronted with bad news. And the worse it is, and the more it affects you personally, the more tempting it is to seek it out, however depressing it might be. A lot of us will have noticed ourselves doing this when Covid first appeared in our lives. It's a perfectly normal and often useful response to look for more information when you're anxious about something. So if you're about to have an operation, you might read up on it, to understand more about what it's going to be like for you. Sometimes having that knowledge will put your mind at rest. But there are occasions where seeking more information doesn't alleviate the uncertainty you feel; it increases it. Presenting two or sometimes three radio programmes on the pandemic every week for nearly two years meant I was steeped in information about it. I read every new scientific paper or finding about the coronavirus, as well as spending my days interviewing virologists and epidemiologists. Alas, it was one of those topics where the more you know, the more you realise how much is unknown, which is hardly reassuring.

So, here's an idea. What about counteracting doom-scrolling online with 'kindness-scrolling'? In other words, how about immersing yourself in good news rather than bad news? Gillian Sandstrom, who's a professor at Sussex University and part of the team behind the Kindness Test, got people to look at a real Twitter feed featuring news on Covid for two minutes, while another group spent the same amount of time looking at the @covidkind Twitter, which was filled with lovely moments of pandemic-related kindness. A third group did nothing. Then they all filled scales measuring mood and optimism. The result? The people who read about the pandemic had lower levels of well-being than those who read tales of kindness, even though the kind stories still concerned Covid. Perhaps not very surprising, but evidence of just how much social media can affect our mood, even when we're only on it for two minutes.

In a second and similar study, people watched four minutes of a YouTuber reacting to negative news about the pandemic, such as doctors not having enough PPE, while others watched the same YouTuber reacting to the news that people were leaving out thank you gifts for delivery drivers. Again well-being was lower if they watched the negative news, but this time average mood was actually improved if they watched the video on kindness towards delivery drivers.[5]

So if just four minutes of hearing about kindness can have this kind of impact on us, what effect could regular time spent kindness-scrolling have? More research will be needed, but it's surely reasonable to speculate that some of the doom and gloom that social media can spread would be alleviated.

And to save you going online to find some kindness, here are some kind acts . . .

LAST ACT OF KINDNESS RECEIVED

The Kindness Test

My daughter did the washing up, because she thought I looked tired.

Airport security personnel allowed ashes of dead to pass through the system unhindered and made sure I got my bag back personally without delay.

Husband forgave me when I was horrid to him.

I really liked a rose at a garden centre but there were five of us in the car and no room. My neighbours returned the next day and bought it for me.

I was made homeless and someone took me in, fed me and washed all my dirty clothes.

On top of a mountain, I took a photo of a couple of hikers. They thanked me for my kindness, which I thought was kindness itself.

A stranger helping me buy a train ticket from a machine.

A surprise delivery of flowers and lovely messages from my line manager.

At a festival I attended on my own a young couple took me under their wing to make sure I was OK and enjoyed myself.

4

KIND PEOPLE CAN BE WINNERS

In one of his most famous novels the great Russian writer Fyodor Dostoyevsky set out with the explicit aim of celebrating a 'positively good and beautiful' man. The title of this novel is *The Idiot*.

The dislocation between aim and title sums up the classic view of kindness – in both literature and life – that kind people may be delightful and lovable, but they're also dupes and fools, who are too good for a harsh world, which will end up destroying them.

Things, it must be said, do not turn out well for Prince Myshkin, the 'idiot' of the title. Dostoyevsky attempts to show that the characters who assume Myshkin's goodness and simplicity denote a lack of human insight and worldly wisdom are wrong. If there is a hero in the book it is him. Yet by the end of the novel one of the women Myshkin loves and tries to protect has been murdered and the other elopes with a fraudster. The murderer, another person Myshkin tries to befriend and help, is sentenced to 15 years hard labour in Siberia, while as for the Prince himself . . . he ends up going mad and is sent back to the sanatorium that he had just left at the start of the story.

As many critics have pointed out, the prince may have set out to do good, but in fact he achieves nothing other than making everyone's life worse – including his own. So much for being kind. Other amiable and kindly figures in great literature – such as Don Quixote and Pickwick – may not cause quite such mayhem and misery as Myshkin, but they are depicted as bumbling and accident prone. The lesson seems to be: if you are naïve and guileless you will come a cropper.

But I want to challenge that view and present the mounting evidence that shows kind people aren't suckers or losers. In fact they are, more often than not, successful people – people who win.

This is because to be kind is not to be soft or gullible, but to be fair and consistent and trustworthy. It is about understanding other people and therefore being able to get the best out of them – crucial for anyone leading a team or running an organisation. And it is about seeing the bigger picture, that success comes not from taking short cuts, still less from ripping people off, but rather as a result of hard work, over a sustained period, weathering the ups and downs.

A tale of three bosses (and two more)

The show I present on Radio 4, *All in the Mind*, covers psychology and neuroscience, and every two years we host the All in the Mind Awards, when people can nominate someone who has supported them through their mental health difficulties. The range of entries that are submitted is wide and varied, from the next-door neighbours who invite in a bereaved parent whenever she needs to talk about her child who died, to the phone shop customer who got chatting to the sales assistant and discovered he was an ex-basketball player finding it difficult to cope with life after his sporting career ended through injury. As part of the judging panel, I sit reading dozens and dozens of stories of exceptional kindness all in a row. I always cry, but as a way of restoring my faith in human nature there's nothing to beat it. In a sense it's a form of kindness-scrolling.

Over the years, the people who've been nominated include partners, relatives, friends, psychologists, nurses, doctors, work colleagues and . . . bosses. These last nominations are among the most moving, not least because they challenge perceptions of the role and characteristics of the boss in modern life. Aren't bosses supposed to be tough and ruthless? Aren't they supposed to care only about efficiency and high performance? Isn't this what TV programmes like *The Apprentice* and *Dragons' Den* tell us is required if you are going to succeed in business? Well, increasingly, it seems these shows are peddling outdated notions.

Before she went to university Rosa worked in a shoe shop. She was brilliant with the customers, friendly, warm and helpful – a natural, her boss Ian said. Everyone at the shop missed her when she went off to university – Ian especially.

But things didn't go well for Rosa at university. She began experiencing symptoms of psychosis, started to believe that she had been chosen by some higher god-like authority and ended up being detained under Section 4 of the Mental Health Act. Rosa received treatment and got better, but didn't feel she could return to university. Instead, she went back home to London and back to her job at the shoe shop. But she'd lost so much confidence because of her illness that at times she would just stand by the racks of shoes shaking uncontrollably, or she would start a sale with a customer and then find herself hyperventilating and would run off halfway through.

Her sanctuary was the basement office. On some days she spent seven hours of every shift crying and panicking in this room. The model employee had become a burden on the rest of the team and a drain on the business. Or that is how some bosses might have viewed the situation. But Ian didn't give up on Rosa. He talked to her and let her sit until she was feeling better. He helped her to face her fears. He was determined to rebuild her confidence, by insisting that she continued coming in to work.

When he was in his twenties, Ian had experienced some anxiety himself after the death of a friend. He knew that what he had needed then was someone to help him through a dark period and this is what he set out to do with Rosa. Gradually she started to spend less time in the office and more time with the customers. Eventually, she was back making a big contribution to the success of the shop. Ian's kindness paid off for Rosa, but also for his business.

Steve runs an IT company where Andrew is one of 400 employees. Andrew experienced bouts of severe depression and sometimes considered suicide, while at other times he had extreme highs and he would spend money he didn't have. He was also very successful at work. He was so fastidious and dogged in negotiations that he won one of the biggest contracts the company had signed in a decade. But sometimes his obsessiveness would become too much and he'd upset clients and other staff.

Andrew was diagnosed with bipolar disorder, but was so worried that he'd lose his job if this was discovered that he hid it from his colleagues. Gradually Steve worked out that Andrew was experiencing serious mental health difficulties, but rather than finding an excuse to get rid of him as a liability to the business, he made it his mission to do everything he could to keep him on.

When Andrew couldn't work for months at a time his job was left open for him, long after Steve could have legally let him go. The financial cost to Steve was considerable. But still he persisted. Andrew says if it wasn't for this kindness he would have lost both his house and his family. And that was partly why Steve acted as he did. But pure altruism wasn't the only reason. Steve also felt it made business sense.

As he said to me: 'It's much cheaper to rehabilitate somebody than it is to recruit someone new. And you never know if the person you recruit might have issues in the future anyway. There's also the message it sends to the rest of the workforce. Every single company contains people with these issues in some shape or form.'

Back in 2018, in Edinburgh, Gillian reached the lowest point of her life. She was in hospital after another suicide attempt, brought on by what she calls a 'perfect storm' of mental health conditions: bipolar disorder, binge eating disorder and premenstrual dysphoric disorder.

When she was discharged from hospital, Gillian's consultant suggested it would help if she looked for work. Gillian had been a special needs teacher before her illness, but thought no one would employ her in such a responsible job now. So she posted on Facebook, saying she was a retired teacher looking for admin work. A nursery school got in touch and invited her for an interview. 'With nothing to lose I put it all out on the table,' Gillian told me. Despite sharing her full history, she was offered a job and the nursery manager, Natalie, said they'd make the necessary adjustments. Gillian thought it was all too good to be true, but Natalie kept to her word, giving her time off when she needed it or cutting her workload.

Gillian's friends and family say they've never known her to be this happy. Gillian says Natalie has given her life back. But surely this generosity and kindness came at a cost to the nursery? Natalie thinks not. She says that Gillian seemed like a lovely person and she knew she had a lot to offer. She says being kind is worth it to create a good atmosphere at work and that when you support staff you get the best from them because they want to work hard. In other words, the kindness is more than repaid.

Now, I do realise that the bosses in these three tales are, in a way, exceptional. After all, they were nominated for an award that specifically recognises compassion. It would be naive to suggest that all or even most bosses are as kind to their vulnerable employees as Natalie, Steve and Ian. But look around the business world and you'll find that there are a growing number of examples of leaders who think it pays to be kind. Here are just two examples.

Graham Allcott runs a successful training company, delivering workshops to large businesses on how to achieve high productivity. You might expect then that productivity in his own business is a top priority for him. And it is, but not at the expense of his staff's well-being, which Graham insists he always puts first.

At one point it seemed so many different traumatic life

events happened to members of his team that Graham used to joke that the business must be cursed. Then he realised this was 'just life', that at some point everyone has relatives who are ill or has home emergencies that need to be sorted out. So now if a staff member needs time off they always get it, with colleagues stepping in to cover, knowing that next time they might be the one to benefit. Graham even allows his staff a small number of 'duvet days' each year when they can choose not to come to work without explaining the reason. They might be feeling sad or tired or even hungover – and that's fine. No explanation needed.

James Timpson is the boss of the highly successful chain offering shoe repairs, key cutting and all manner of other services. In 2019 (before the pandemic hit) the Timpson Group reported turnover of £300 million and profits of more than £20 million. And yet the company has a highly ethical approach to business, most famously employing ex-prisoners, giving them the training and support they need to reintegrate back into society. Ex-offenders make up 10% of Timpson's workforce and the company is justifiably proud of this record. But they don't do it just out of the goodness of their hearts. As their website says: 'The vast majority of ex-offenders we recruit are extremely loyal, productive, hardworking and make excellent colleagues. Many have been promoted and fully grasped the second chance they have been given. To put it simply, recruiting ex-offenders has been great for our business.'

The question remains though as to whether these kind bosses are exceptional rather than the norm. The evidence, inevitably, is somewhat mixed.

In the Kindness Test, people were asked where they most

often see acts of kindness taking place. Home came first, followed by medical settings, and I think we'd probably all agree that it's right that they score so high. But after that? The next place where people observed kind acts was in the workplace. It was also the place, again after home and hospitals, where people felt kindness was truly valued. As for the fields people work in, those in social work, healthcare, hospitality and education felt kindness was valued the most, which is intriguing when those are the fields where people often tell me they no longer have the time to be as kind as they'd like to, because they are under so much pressure.

The fact that in general people do feel that kindness is valued at work is encouraging. But some findings from other studies are less positive. For instance, when a representative sample of a thousand people working in the UK were asked by a branding strategy consultancy for their views on kindness, only one in three strongly agreed that their immediate boss was kind and only one in four considered the leader of their whole organisation to be kind.[1] So far, so gloomy. But those respondents who did have kind bosses were more likely to intend to stay at their company for at least another year, to say that their team produces outstanding work and to say their company was doing well financially.

We can't conclude definitively that because a leader is kind, their company does well. Perhaps these kind leaders also have other skills which make their organisations successful. Even so there are positive signs here. And leaders with whom this same branding strategy consultancy works, ranging from handbag designer Anya Hindmarch to the chief constable of Avon and Somerset Police, all insisted that acting kindly has resulted in better performances from staff, while fully

96% of the employees that took part in the survey said that being kind at work is important to them.

Of course, there are certainly still many leaders around who are successful through taking a ruthless approach to business and driving their employees hard. There are plenty of workplaces where staff have little autonomy and are on low pay and zero-hours contracts. But the point is that this isn't the only way to succeed, and a kinder business style is growing in popularity. One of the reasons for this is that the new cohort of leaders includes young people, more women, more people from diverse backgrounds, all of whom are less attached to old, macho styles of management. As we'll see in Chapter 7, an important part of being more kind is being kinder to yourself, and this idea too is spreading in the business world, overturning notions that success only comes with long hours, a relentless focus on work and a monomaniacal commitment to the company.

For example, Whitney Wolfe Herd is a self-made female billionaire, a very select club, which she joined at the age of just 31. She runs the dating agency Bumble, which puts women in charge of making the first contact with potential partners. She says she used to be a workaholic who'd wake up every two hours to check her inbox, but speaking to the BBC's *CEO Secrets* programme she said she was now making more time for family and friends and living a more rounded life: 'The one piece of advice I wish I had when I started out would be to not take yourself too seriously . . . Work is amazing and finding success is very rewarding but there is no reward in the end if you neglect the things that matter the most. So, it is incredibly important, regardless of how tired or busy or overloaded you are in your day to day, you must make time to call your grandparents or call an old friend.'

Kind not soft

Being a kind boss is not the same thing as being a soft boss. It is important to stress that. In the examples above, we saw instances where managers allowed employees to take time off work, but that was in exceptional circumstances (notably, because of mental ill health) and the bosses acted the way they did because they calculated (rightly) that their generosity would be repaid with hard work from these employees in the future. Sending everyone home for the afternoon every time it's sunny or giving everyone a big Christmas bonus despite declining sales might well run a business into the ground. Instead, a kind boss needs to create an environment in which their staff can all get the most out of their jobs, giving them the freedom to work in the way that suits them best. And they do this because countless studies show that greater autonomy leads to higher job satisfaction and higher job satisfaction leads to greater productivity.

At Kindfest, the festival held every year to celebrate World Kindness Day, Nicholas de Wolff, who is a strategic advisor to many businesses, including those in the film industry, told an audience that if kindness was seen as disruptive and damaging, then CEOs would of course be right to resist it. He said: 'I need to convince them it's a stepping stone to survival, not a burden or a challenge.' Kindness, he said, certainly doesn't mean letting everyone slack off.

But it does involve sincere generosity and consideration

of others, creating an atmosphere in which everyone feels connected, which in turn makes people happier in their work.[2] Another important factor is generating a sense that everyone is working towards a shared goal. This increases staff motivation and generates loyalty to the company. By contrast, putting more and more pressure on staff doesn't increase performance. Kind leaders are allowed to give up on relationships that don't work (i.e. fire people, ultimately) but they should give their staff every chance to improve performance. They can care for others, but also stand up for themselves and their organisation.

When it comes to the evidence, much of the academic research in this area takes place within a fairly new field of research called ethical leadership. (It seems that is an easier phrase for some in business to get on board with than 'kind leadership'.)

This requires leaders to invest high levels of trust in their staff, which in turn promotes cohesion – though without people feeling they must agree all the time. Ethical leaders are scored highly by their staff on two of the so-called Big Five personality factors most closely aligned to kindness – agreeableness and conscientiousness.[3] Which is all very nice, perhaps, but does it achieve results? A 2013 study suggests it does.

Joe Folkman who is a psychometrician (someone who does psychometric testing) in the US, studied the 360-degree feedback ratings of more than 50,000 leaders and found the more likeable leaders tended also to be rated highly on effectiveness by their staff. His called his study: 'I'm the boss. Why should I care if you like me?'[4] The answer is that they should care – and care a lot – if they want to be good at their jobs. In fact Folkman found that to score low on like-ability, yet high on effectiveness, was so rare that there was only a one in 2,000 chance of it happening. His team have continued to collect data in the intervening years and Folkman re-ran the figures for my BBC series *The Anatomy of Kindness*, this time with ratings for more than 100,000 leaders, and the results showed that being a great boss, but not very likeable, has become even rarer. Folkman also showed that the likeable leaders score higher on a whole range of outcomes, including profitability and customer satisfaction.

Other studies have shown that ethical leadership results in a more positive and collaborative atmosphere at work and, crucially, that employees perform better too.[5] Another advantage of this style of leadership is that it doesn't require high levels of charisma or extraversion, both of which are difficult traits for people to learn if they don't come naturally. This means the field of leadership is opened up to a wider range of candidates.

The psychologist Michael Brown has studied ethical leadership in depth and found that when leaders behave ethically, staff are more likely to speak up about important issues and to take risks instead of taking the safe option.[6] An ethical leader encourages a sense among their employees that working for the company is not just a purely economic transaction, but a social endeavour, which encourages staff to work harder towards greater shared success. Having said that, becoming the ideal ethical leader sounds quite demanding. Michael told me they need to be principled, humble, open to feedback and prepared to be role models for everyone else. Oh, and of course they need to run the organisation too.

Within psychology, social learning theory has demon-strated time and again that we often copy the behaviour we see in others. So if the boss shows kindness and considera-tion, this behaviour can cascade through the company. To demonstrate this the well-known social psychologist Jonathan Haidt conducted a study in a leading Italian furniture company that makes wooden doors for houses, asking staff to fill in anonymous questionnaires and drop them in a box in reception. It included the tale of a fictional boss called Massimo Castelli who'd recently taken charge of a marble and granite company. The staff were asked to imagine that they worked for this other made-up company and that they feared losing their job because many clients had started buying from cheaper competitors. In one version of the story Signor Castelli stopped informing his managers and staff of his decisions, rarely held meetings and was generally unkind. In another version, he put in no extra effort, apart from trying to open up opportunities for himself. In a third version, his door was always open, he was very fair with the staff and asked for their patience during the company's difficulties. Then in a final version, he took a pay cut and even invested his own money in the company in an attempt to save it.[7]

You'll not be surprised to learn that respondents said that just reading this last story made them feel more altruistic, courteous and committed to the future of the imaginary business. And of course the likelihood is that if this feeling was converted into actual work for the struggling company its chances of survival would be better. Signor Castelli was therefore acting not just in a kind way, but in a smart way.

But of course the example here was hypothetical. What would happen in real life? To follow up, Haidt and his team went to a public hospital near the Italian city of Padua. Nurses were asked confidential questions about their actual bosses. Did they stand up for the team? Were they fair? Were they self-sacrificing? In cases where the answers were positive, the nurses felt what Haidt describes as 'morally elevated' and they reported more often the desire to do something good for someone else, to be like their boss or to become a better person.

Kindness can of course be extended to clients and customers too – and with similarly positive results. I'm lucky enough to have a local bike shop where, instead of the guys there patronising me for not knowing how to mend my own bike (which has happened elsewhere), they are friendly and understanding and – more to the point – sometimes do a quick repair without even charging me. I now love this shop and when I want to buy something like panniers or bike lights or a new helmet I don't look online, I go to the local bike shop – even though their prices are a bit higher. And when I need a new bike one day, I know where I'm going first. So, although the shop perhaps loses out on the odd fiver or tenner for the two-minute job of fixing my bike seat or mending a puncture, they've won a loyal customer who will spend much more than that over the coming years.

All in all, the evidence shows that being a kind person in business is not a barrier to success. Indeed, the opposite can be true. But a recent bestselling book does give me pause. Its title is *Nice Girls Don't Get the Corner Office* and it speaks to the need for women to be assertive if they are to get on. So, as a feminist who's furious about the enduring gap between men's and women's pay and the continuing lack of women in boardrooms, I worry that advising women who want to succeed to be even kinder at work could be misinterpreted.

Dr Marcia Sirota, the psychotherapist and founder of the Ruthless Compassion Institute, writes in *Be Kind, Not Nice* that people can sometimes become so keen to please that they'll do anything for anyone, hoping to be liked for it, only to become frustrated in the end because they feel unappreciated and their efforts aren't rewarded and others start taking their niceness for granted. This is often true of women, I think, partly because of the way we are brought up and treated at school.

But Lauren Currie, who runs a leadership development company called Stride, which specialises in empowering women to succeed in the workplace, remains convinced that the kindness of many women can give them 'an invisible competitive advantage'. She makes a distinction between kindness and being nice, though, and argues that it is niceness in women that gets weaponised against them, not kindness.

In this area, the distinction between niceness and kindness comes up a lot, with being nice coming in for a bad rap. Marcia Sirota goes as far as to suggest that being nice is insincere because people only do it to win approval from others. It can, she says, result in constantly seeking to people-please and wanting to avoid confrontation for fear of causing upset or being rejected. This in turn can make others see your niceness as attention-seeking and lead them to see you as a doormat. By contrast, the kind person is being loved for who they are, Marcia says, and their favours don't feel as though they come with strings attached.

I'm not sure the distinction is as clear as that. I think

kindness and niceness intersect. Helping someone pick up their dropped shopping is both a nice act and a kind one, to take just one obvious example. But where Marcia and others are onto something is that kind acts can happen without looking for approval and don't always involve meekness or weakness. A kind boss doesn't let one person get away with slacking while others take on their work because in the long run that's not kind to anyone involved. Kindness can involve difficult conversations and tough decisions, as long as these are undertaken fairly and reasonably. Acting kindly doesn't mean always putting everyone else first. A kind workplace is one where everyone feels valued and fairly treated, not one where bosses don't stand up to people.

As well as practising kindness, a good leader needs to preach it. Michael Brown has found that for ethical leadership to have a real impact on staff, it needs to be very noticeable, and it's not enough for the boss just to behave ethically in his or her personal dealings. In other words, a leader needs to be explicit about kindness and inculcate it as a big part of the company culture. Kindness needs to be – dare I say it? – part of the 'brand'.

By now, I might have convinced you that kindness at work is effective when things are going well, but what about when they aren't? Sometimes a boss has to make a difficult or unpopular decision that their staff – or some of them, at least – won't like. A leader might want to appear agreeable at all times, but that is not always possible or even desirable. The nice version of Massimo Castelli may have been willing to cut his own salary to save the business, but sometimes pay freezes or redundancies are necessary if the company is to survive. Sometimes, a particular member of staff has behaved so badly, or performed so badly, they have to be sacked, not least to be kind to the rest of their colleagues. In both cases, it is not kind for a boss to duck making difficult calls. A good leader in these circumstances will act with transparency, objectivity, fairness and decisiveness.

A friend of mine, who has had to dismiss people on several occasions, even goes so far as to say that firing someone can be an act of kindness. Poor performance, he says, can often result from a person being in a job that is too much for them, and so relieving them of their post in this situation can lead to them finding another job elsewhere that suits them better. And there are also occasions where the rest of the team has to take on the work of a colleague who persistently fails to pull their weight. A manager who tackles this problem may not be popular with that particular staff member, but is showing compassion towards the rest of the team if they can sort out the situation.

Soft-hearted triathletes, ethical footballers and a very considerate foreign correspondent

So far in this chapter, I've focused mainly on business, but elite sport is another cut-throat arena in which looking out for number one may seem to be the only way to win. And, yes, on the whole that is true. If you have the chance of a last-minute penalty to win the cup final then it generally isn't the done thing to shoot wide of the goal out of kindness to your opponents. No, you smash the ball into the back of the net and break the other team's hearts. Get over it!

And yet even in sport, there are instances of kindness and

self-sacrifice that can make a competitor a winner in a different way. Take Diego Méntrida. He is a top tier triathlete, which means that physically he is a hard man, capable of competing in the higher echelons of a brutal event. But that doesn't mean he isn't also a kind and considerate man.

This side of Diego was demonstrated in an incident that attracted global attention in September 2020. In a triathlon in his native Spain, Méntrida was coming in fourth behind a British athlete, James Teagle, when, with just 100 metres to go to the finish line, Teagle took a wrong turn. This left Méntrida free to run through and claim a bronze medal. But he didn't do that. Instead he slowed down, let Teagle catch up and run in ahead of him. He did it, Méntrida later explained, because Teagle 'deserved to win'.

Lovely story, but I've said kind people can be winners, and Méntrida was surely the loser, wasn't he? Well, not if you think about it. As I say, his kind gesture attracted global attention, raising Diego's own profile – which he may or may not have enjoyed – but also the profile of his sport – which he doubtless did welcome. The triathlon was sponsored by the Spanish bank Santander, and I'm sure the publicity around Diego's actions delighted them, perhaps helping to ensure that their sponsorship of triathlons continued. It was even reported that Méntrida was awarded an honorary third place by the organisers and the same €300 (£274) prize money as Teagle.[8] So, although Méntrida lost out on third place in one race, he gained in so many other ways.

This tale might bring to mind for you another more famous instance of triathletic kindness. This time an example of brotherly love, even though the two brothers in question are fierce rivals in their chosen sport.

Jonny Brownlee was leading with just 700 metres to go at the end of the World Triathlon Series in Mexico in 2016. Victory in this race would have given Jonny the world title. But at this point he suddenly started to weave and wobble, to swerve and stumble, in the extremely hot and humid conditions. He was clearly in great physical distress.

Jonny's elder brother, Alistair, was coming in third at the time, but abandoning his own chances of a victory, put his arm around his sibling, propped him up, and pushed him over the line in second place, with another competitor racing past to take victory.

All this meant that Jonny also just missed out on the world title, while Alistair came 10th in the final standings. But who, in the wider scheme, ended up being the winner from this episode? The 2016 champion Mario Mola certainly didn't think it was him, saying his success had been overshadowed and it wasn't how he would have wanted to win the championships. I would suggest that the real winner was, in fact, Alistair Brownlee. He may have won two Olympic golds, been Triathlon World Champion twice, European champion four times, but surely this was his finest hour?

I mentioned football at the top of this section and it is generally regarded as a sport that rewards a ruthless 'win at all costs' mentality. At least until recently, the model for a top manager in the sport has been Sir Alex Ferguson, famous for giving his underperforming players the 'hairdryer treatment', or José Mourinho, with his brand of megalomaniac charisma and high-octane motivational skills. Yet during the 2020 Euro championships – which because of the pandemic actually took place in 2021 – a very different approach to football was demonstrably successful, if not quite successful enough to win the final.

The England football team manager, Gareth Southgate, is a softly spoken and calm man, who seems genuinely concerned about his players' mental well-being, as well as their form on the field. He fostered a culture of kindness in his team, perhaps giving scope for stars such as Marcus Rashford to act publicly on the social issues they felt strongly about – in Rashford's case campaigning against child poverty and for free school meals to be distributed through the school holidays. Southgate stood up for the decision by his team to take the knee at the start of each match as a symbol of anti-racism, despite the abuse and boos they received from some of their own fans. Then in the Euro final his team took part in a very public act of kindness out on the pitch, physically forming a circle around the young Black footballers who had just missed penalties, thereby losing England the champion-ship. The other players were shielding their teammates from the crowds and the cameras, perhaps guessing the degree of the racist abuse they would soon be enduring on social media. And Southgate isn't afraid to admit to valuing kindness either, naming his own book *Anything Is Possible: Be Brave, Be Kind and Follow Your Dreams*.

The sports psychologist Michael Caulfield described Southgate's approach as involving 'empathy, kindness and understanding. He's highly competitive and can be quite ruth-less, but that doesn't stop you being decent at the same time; he's giving a modern lesson in decency at the moment.'[9]

OK, as I say, in the end England didn't end up winning the tournament, but they came closer than they had in a generation and in the process showed there is another way to succeed, even in the ruthless world of football. As Marcus Rashford himself put it on Twitter: 'always remember that kindness is power'.

Kindness can foster team spirit while the opposite, rudeness, dampens our trust in our colleagues and serves to demotivate us. The effects might be so small that bosses don't even notice, but they matter. Whether or not you know the psychological name for them, assuming you're a kind person, then at work you carry out 'organisational citizenship behaviours'. Reporting the printer as broken, rather than just leaving it for the next poor person to discover, watering the plants, being helpful. These small actions on behalf of all your colleagues keep things going and make working life easier for everyone. But as soon as we begin to feel that we're not being treated fairly because of unequal pay or a sense that our work is unappreciated or that bosses are behaving unethically, we withdraw these behaviours. We don't sort out the broken printer, because why should we?

Once again unkindness begets unkindness and kindness begets kindness.

Dozens of studies have been done on the impact of organisational citizenship behaviours and they can give us a window onto the impact of kind behaviour at work.

In a 2009 meta-analysis by a researcher at the University of Arizona called Nathan Podsakoff of more than 150 different studies involving 51,000 people, these behaviours have been shown to have a real impact.[10] They do much more than foster a friendly atmosphere. A high frequency of kind acts like these correlates positively with job performance, productivity, customer satisfaction and efficiency. Where people don't help each other out in this way, absenteeism is higher and more people consider leaving. So kindness really does matter.

Finally I want to mention another kind winner in a field that is also generally considered to be ruthlessly competitive – journalism. As I've mentioned already, I keep a Kindness Diary and I was struck by an entry from March 2022, a couple of weeks after Russia invaded Ukraine:

> *Was just scrolling through Twitter and I see that one of the BBC's most successful correspondents, Lyse Doucet, has tweeted a photo of five of the people she's working with in Ukraine, saying: 'OUR TEAM – these are some of the great people behind the cameras in #Kyiv who make all the difference. Huge thanks.' And then a list of their names.*

Lyse Doucet is well known within the BBC for repeatedly sharing the credit with those working behind the scenes – not something all high-profile, on-air journalists do. And yet this kindness clearly hasn't held her back, since she has succeeded in becoming the Chief International Correspondent.

Learning from Lady Montagu

Let's turn to perhaps the most cut-throat professional arena of all – politics. Surely it is without question a venomous snake pit and no place for decency and kindness? Think again. In fact, even in politics, research shows it pays to be a good guy. In fact, I say good guy, but it took a good gal to first notice this, a remarkable woman called Lady Mary Wortley Montagu who died in 1762. (Do look her up, she should be better known.) What Lady Montagu observed is that 'civility costs nothing and buys everything'. This is now known as the Montagu Principle which, very simply put, proposes that behaving badly does not – in the long term at least – lead to success in politics.

So do all politicians always abide by the Montagu Principle? Of course not. But even the most unlikely politicians at least give a nod to it. Former President Trump, for instance, is among those who have called for more civility in politics.[11] What Trump recognised perhaps is that numerous political studies have shown that negative campaigning tends to back-fire. It wins you attention, but it doesn't make people like you, or more importantly vote for you. Perhaps he should have taken his own advice; we know what happened to him in the end (as I write anyway).

Between 1996 and 2015, the academic Jeremy Frimer analysed the language used by members of the US Congress during floor debates. In his study, he showed that Congress members' approval ratings went down when they were uncivil in their speeches in the House, and up when they were polite and generous. The more civil politicians also showed their astuteness because their higher approval ratings prompted them to behave even more politely, thereby increasing their ratings even more.[12]

Once Donald Trump came along, Frimer's team couldn't resist analysing Trump's tweets (this was before The Donald was banned from Twitter of course). What better pool of data to look at, after all? It was spontaneously generated and free for anyone to see. Not surprisingly, Frimer found that people who were not Trump supporters disapproved of him even more when he was being rude or hateful. But what was more striking was that very few of his supporters actively *liked* his nastier tweets. The tweets didn't stop them supporting him, but they carried on doing so *despite*, not because of, his incivility. In one interesting example, these supporters indicated that when their man was attacked by journalists they preferred him to change the subject rather than go on the offensive.

In complete contrast to Donald Trump, the Prime Minister of New Zealand Jacinda Ardern says in her book *I Know This to Be True* that of all the qualities that have underpinned her path to becoming the prime minister of New Zealand, the most important has been kindness. 'I think one of the sad things that I've seen in political leadership is – because we've placed over time so much emphasis on notions of assertiveness and strength – that we probably have assumed that it means you can't have those other qualities of kindness and empathy. And yet, when you think about all the big challenges that we face in the world, that's probably the quality we need the most.'

Ardern says we need our leaders to be able to empathise with the circumstances of others, and also with the next generation. She says we mustn't focus on being the most powerful person in the room. She is proud to focus on empathy, because she is convinced you can be 'both empathetic and strong.'

Of course, like anywhere New Zealand has it problems and Ardern is by no means universally popular, but by any standards she has been a successful leader, notably in steering her country through the global pandemic. And although it is of course easier to deal with a virus on a small island that's geographically situated far away from most of the world than in a huge country, the contrast with Donald Trump's disastrous handling of Covid-19 in the US is striking.

When members of the general public in Belgium were asked in 2009 to imagine the traits that an ideal politician would have, traits associated with kindness scored highly. Conscientiousness was considered the most important quality of all, but agreeableness came joint second. When the same researchers looked at more detailed personality characteristics, friendliness was rated as more important in a politician than drive, moderation or 'poise and polish'. Machiavellianism came way down, close to the bottom of the list, and was unpopular all round, and even more so with left-wing voters.[13]

As ever with research of this sort, the conclusions that can be drawn must be somewhat tentative. Studies do not show definitively that being kindly is a hugely popular quality in all politicians all of the time. And just look at politicians like Vladimir Putin, Jair Bolsonaro and Rodrigo Duterte – all ruthless men, all very popular with swathes of their electorates. But on the other hand, there are gentler, more empathic, politicians – forgive me if I tend to highlight *female* politicians – who have shown there is a different path to political success, not just Jacinda Ahern, but also Angela Merkel and Nicola Sturgeon.

Nice Phil wins

This chapter started with an example from classic literature, but I'm going to end it with TV comedy. *Modern Family* is classic comfort-viewing. In this hugely successful series, which ran from 2009 to 2020, we follow the lives of three different families, all related to each other. One family comprises an older white man, his much younger Latina wife and their two sons. Another family is made up of two gay white men and their adopted Vietnamese daughter. And the third family is a classic nuclear family: Dad and Mom and three children.

The father of the third family – Phil Dunphy – is a quintessential 'nice guy'. A bit nerdy and goofy, a big kid at heart. By contrast, the father of the first family, Jay Pritchett – who is Phil's father-in-law – is a grumpy, no-nonsense, hardheaded business man. Jay always thinks he can cut the best deals and is rather dismissive of Phil, who he sees as weak.

In an episode in series six that I watched recently, Phil shows typical kindness towards his self-obsessed eldest daughter Haley by buying her a car for her 21st birthday. He has got a good deal, but when Jay hears about it, he tries to take over, assuming that Phil will have been too soft and conciliatory with the car dealers and so will have been cheated on the price. He takes a tough negotiating stance, convinced he'll win out.

In many Hollywood shows, this would indeed be the result. But this time – and more in line with reality, I'd argue – Jay's approach results in the original deal falling through. Phil's more trusting and collaborative approach was the better one. All is resolved happily in the end – Haley gets her car. But the message from this show – a welcome one – is that sometimes the best wheeler-dealing comes from playing it straight rather than going in for hardball. In other words, the kind person can come out on top.

LAST KIND ACT CARRIED OUT FOR SOMEONE ELSE

The Kindness Test

I carried a pushchair over a very muddy part of a path for a young mother.

My five-year-old grandson was collecting stones of various different types and I helped him organise them carefully.

I bought some new clothes for Afghan refugees yesterday.

Walking. Dog ran up to me and made me dirty. Owner very apologetic. Had a nice chat about the morning. Wanted to make owner feel good.

Driving to the beach (I hate beaches).

Gave some tomatoes I'd grown to a neighbour after having an argument with her.

I talked to a lonely person at my club. She said I had made her day.

I cleaned up a dear friend after she'd suffered double incontinence.

My brother is bipolar and lives alone. He said his mattress was very hard and he wasn't sleeping well. I ordered a memory foam mattress topper for him.

Unprompted admiration of a good dog in a pub garden.

5

KINDNESS COMES FROM SEEING OTHER PEOPLE'S POINTS OF VIEW

"Atticus, he was real nice . . ." . . . "Most people are, Scout, when you finally see them." This exchange comes on the final page of the one of the most popular books in publishing history: *To Kill a Mockingbird* by Harper Lee. Atticus Finch has been reading a story to his daughter, Scout, a story that features a misunderstood character called Stoner's Boy. To readers of the novel, it is clear that Stoner's Boy symbolises the Finches' neighbour Boo Radley.

Boo is an oddball and a recluse, and is treated with suspicion and hostility by others in Maycomb, Alabama, the fictional setting for the novel. Influenced by this general view, the Finch children, Jem and Scout, make up wild and horrific stories about Boo and believe that he murders people's pets. To begin with, they make no effort to understand Boo or to see things from his perspective. But as the novel progresses, the children come to empathise with him and realise that he is in fact kind and protective towards them.

Scout and Jem make this journey partly because they have a great role model in their father, Atticus, who must be one of the kindest ever characters in literature. He sees good in everyone, even racist neighbours like Mrs Dubose or the truly despicable Bob Ewell. Indeed, as with Prince Myshkin in Chapter 4 of this book, Atticus's generous attitude can at times be recklessly naive, even putting his children in danger, so determined is he to see the best in people. But overall, his kindly outlook wins the day, and the message from Harper Lee's novel is very clear: we would all benefit if we followed Atticus's example and were more tolerant and empathic in our attitudes to others.

It's a message I'm sure most of us would agree with, and yet in the years since *To Kill a Mockingbird* was published in 1960, it might seem as if our willingness to see things from other people's point of view has diminished rather than increased. Certainly, public discourse, amplified by social media, suggests that we are ever more entrenched in our more polarised viewpoints, only engaging with people with different views in order to hurl abuse and vitriol at them. We seem to have learned nothing from William Hazlitt who, writing in the nineteenth century, wisely observed: 'If railing would have made it [the world] better, it would have been reformed long ago ... The worst fault it has is want of charity: & calling 'knave' & 'fool' at every turn will not cure this failing.'[1]

I suspect that in our daily lives there is in fact more tolerance and empathy around than we sometimes think. I certainly hope this is true, because I strongly believe that Atticus was right: in almost all cases, people really are 'real nice' if you 'finally see them'. It is just a case – though of course this isn't always easy in practice – of looking beyond your own prejudices and standpoints and appreciating that the views of others matter in a different way.

Essential empathy

The psychologist David Canter is famous for developing the technique of offender profiling and for studying what moti- vates criminals. Newspaper headline writers sometimes dub him 'the real Cracker' – a reference to the lead character, a forensic psychologist played by Robbie Coltrane, in the 1990s TV drama series. Less well known is the fact that Professor Canter studies kindness, and one of his contributions to the field is a useful division of kindness into three sub-types: benign tolerance, empathic responsivity and principled proaction (deliberately instigating kind actions). In this chapter we will be focusing on the second of these sub-types: empathic responsivity.

Now, as I said in the introduction, within academia, debate rages about the exact meaning of certain words, and that goes for 'empathy' as much as others. To complicate (or maybe enrich?) things further, the term empathy can itself be sub-divided. First there is 'cognitive empathy' which is where you try to read someone's mind in order to understand their thoughts, wishes, knowledge, beliefs, perceptions or intentions. Through this process – also known in psychology as 'mentalising' – you attempt to work out what other people are thinking and feeling, without actually thinking or feeling the same way yourself. Then there is 'emotional empathy' where you share another person's feelings more viscerally, where you witness their emotional distress or joy, and at least to some extent 'feel' it as they do.

Put this way, it might seem they are quite different responses – one fairly hard-headed and the other rather soft-hearted; one quite intellectual, the other more instinctive. But in daily life we don't generally distinguish clearly between cognitive and emotional empathy. For instance, if I see a young lone woman crying on the train late at night, I might think that she's just had a row or been dumped. I know what it is *like* to be in her situation as I've been in it myself – and in that sense I 'feel her pain'. But at the same time, I am not *in* her situation now – so I remain at some distance from the anguish she is feeling at that moment. The Harvard psychologist and author Paul Bloom suggests that these types of empathy are 'layered' rather than distinct. When we show empathy, we move seamlessly between the layers, without being conscious of it, rather than clicking mechanically from Cognitive to Emotional. Only rarely is a person able to completely compartmentalise the types of empathy they are deploying, an extreme example being the psychopathic torturer who is able to put themselves inside the mind of their victim in order to manipulate them cruelly, while in no sense feeling for themselves the pain they are inflicting.

Neuroscientific studies show that in most of us – who aren't psychopaths – there is similar neural activity in both a person experiencing physical pain and a person who is only watching someone else in pain. The German psychologist Tania Singer is a leading figure in this area. In a typical experiment she might put someone into a brain scanner and then jab them with a pin (they give their permission for this to happen, I hasten to add), then at other times the person is shown a video of someone else being jabbed with a pin. In both cases, two specific parts of the brain (a portion of the anterior insula and a specific part of the anterior cingulate cortex) tend to be activated, regardless of whether the painful experience was real or vicarious.[2] (Incidentally, there are similar overlaps in brain activity when people are touched or simply watching others being touched, or whether they taste something strong or watch someone else tasting something strong.) What this shows is that our brains seem to allow us to feel emotionally what others are feeling physically. We suffer along with their suffering because we can imagine ourselves in their place. And this effect is particularly marked if the person in pain is someone we can relate to because they're in the same group as us – an example might be someone who supports the same football team.[3]

So strong is the sense of empathy in most of us, that in situations where we experience a palpable absence of empathy from others, we soon start to feel stressed. Indeed, the standard way of inducing stress in laboratory conditions involves a panel of volunteers sitting stony-faced while another participant in the experiment tells them why they'd be a good candidate for a job. It's called the Trier Social Stress Test.

'You should speak for the entire five-minute time period,' a research assistant tells the 'job applicant' in an ante-room before the test starts. Then, without giving the applicant any time to prepare, the assistant adds: 'Please enter the room. Your time begins now.'[4]

Meanwhile the 'interview panel' has been given their

instructions. 'Whatever you do, don't move a muscle. Not a nod, not a twitch, and certainly not a smile. Nothing to show that you have understood or even heard the applicant.' It is such an alien and artificial way to behave that even panel members tend to find the exercise difficult and need to be trained to perform it successfully. But if they do – and the whole thing is captured on video to add to the tension – the clear result is that the person facing the panel experiences severe stress. They simply can't cope with the total lack of empathy shown towards them.⁵

There are many situations in real life that are similar, if perhaps not quite as extreme, as the Trier Social Stress Test. Think of stand-up comedians, particularly warm-up acts, desperately trying to wring a laugh out of punters who are just waiting for the headliner to come on stage. Then there is the phenomenon of 'ghosting' in which you find the person you've been dating has completely cut off contact, without any warning or explanation. Being dumped is bad enough, but this abrupt blanking by a person you may have felt you were getting on with quite well can be especially distressing. Usually, and fortunately, other people do not treat us this way; instead we get a lot back from our interactions with others – and we feed off the reassurance that this under-standing provides.

One of the reasons why working from home during the pandemic has been so gruelling for many is that meetings that would have taken place in person have been transferred online. Instead of being in a room filled with expressive and usually supportive colleagues we've been confronted with galleries of apparently impassive faces trapped in their squares. For most of 2020 and 2021, all the public lectures

I gave were online. To help me through the deadening experience of talking to a virtual and seemingly unresponsive audience, I resorted to scanning the audience members with cameras on and choosing the most smiley person, or even a static photo of someone smiling, to have in my eye-line to avoid accidentally recreating my own personal Trier Social Stress Test.

Our struggle to cope with the lack of an empathic response in others starts in early childhood with babies quickly showing acute distress if their parent looks at them in a cold and expressionless way instead of smiling and cooing. And just as we hate it when the person before us doesn't seem to understand us, we love it when they do. We develop better connections with these people and through those we learn to understand other people's thoughts and feelings, and as a result we return the favour. A virtuous circle of empathy is created and keeps spinning.

But this is the good outcome. Sometimes the circle spins the other way, and in these situations, we need help to understand others.

Professor Peter Fonagy, a psychoanalyst and psychotherapist, has developed a type of psychotherapy called Mentalisation-based treatment or MBT. MBT can be useful for people who find relationships difficult, who tend to mistrust other people and have difficulty in reading other people's responses. During sessions, clients focus on the difficulties in their own life, first to improve their understanding of themselves, but also – and importantly – their understanding of others. Professor Fonagy argues that to be truly kind towards others we have to be able to see things from their perspective, but this is a behaviour that some of us find challenging, hence the need for therapy. When parents make an effort to teach their children – who initially can be suspicious of others – to socialise with other children, or to say hello to neighbours, they're not just helping them to play or to have good manners. They're also – albeit implicitly – inculcating the notion that other people can be trusted, that they are 'like you'. We do have to be vigilant in our interactions with others, Fonagy says, because of course not every single individual is to be trusted, but that vigilance and suspicion mustn't be allowed to dominate our lives.[6]

Of course, most of us are happy to *say* that we think it is important to see other people's perspectives. Who wouldn't agree with that? Everyone's entitled to their opinion after all. But then we can struggle to maintain this stance when we meet someone whose views we fundamentally disagree with.

I, for instance, am convinced (backed by plenty of scientific evidence, I might add) that vaccination against the Covid-19 virus is a good idea. More than that, I think it's been essential in order to escape the worst consequences of the pandemic. As well as presenting radio shows and podcasts on psychology, as I've said I present two BBC World Service programmes on global health. That meant following the new research daily throughout the pandemic. I remember literally skipping for joy when I learned that the results of the very first vaccine trial were to be announced publicly that afternoon – and that the vaccine had worked. After hosting more than 150 programmes on Covid, and having been lucky enough to interview some of the people who developed the vaccines, I'm absolutely convinced that SARS-CoV-2 exists and that the small risks of being vaccinated are massively outweighed by the risks of not getting vaccinated. Yet I know that there are people who are just as convinced that I'm wrong. And a few of them are people I know, people who are intelligent, decent and, yes, kind.

This latter group – and my response to them – should help me to feel more empathy towards anti-vaxxers who I don't know, for in the case of people I do know I am much more prepared to forgive or tolerate their views on vaccines, to 'agree to disagree', without falling out. This is because I can more easily see their perspective, if not on this issue, then on other issues. Indeed, in many instances, I know we share the *same* views and that generally these people are reasonable and pleasant. But with people I don't know personally – notably people sounding off on social media – I fall into the trap of assuming that their ideas about vaccines, which I do genuinely view as profoundly wrong, makes them an idiot, and worse, a bad idiot. I can't balance my opinion of them based on this one issue against my opinion of them based on others.

This leads me to a simple tip for being a kinder person on social media. Before you respond angrily to a post that you strongly disagree with, think to yourself how you would react if the post had come from a friend. I'm guessing you would moderate your response in this case, so why not do so in all situations? After all, there is more than enough 'calling knave and fool' on Twitter and other platforms without any of us adding to it.

More than a walk in someone else's shoes

In an era of polarisation of political views, social media bubbles and echo chambers, it's often said that to understand different viewpoints we should 'put ourselves in other peoples' shoes'. But does this really work? I'm reminded of the joke that starts with the line: 'If I walked a mile in another man's shoes . . .' and ends by adding, 'I'd have some new shoes and I'd be a mile away.' Somehow just donning different metaphorical footwear doesn't feel sufficient to engender significant empathy.

Studies by Paul Gilbert, a psychologist from the University of Derby, who developed compassion-focused therapy, confirm this suspicion. Gilbert has demonstrated that essentially passive techniques – simply plonking yourself in the position of a person you disagree with – rarely lead you to change your mind about that person's views.

What is more successful is arguing your way into their mindset by actively trying to generate lines of argument another person might give to explain their views. This is known as perspective-taking and it's been used to improve understanding between people who vote for diametrically opposed political parties and to create harmony between groups who strongly disapprove of each other's social activities.

In the case of my suspicion of anti-vaxxers, perspective-taking would require me to consider where their mistrust of medical authorities and governments comes from, whether they have been let down by doctors and scientists in the past, and where they are obtaining their information. If they have experienced discrimination from health services, as many people of colour have, for example, and if they have cause to distrust official scientific sources, I can begin to see how they came to view vaccines with suspicion.

From this vantage point, it should become obvious that telling people they're stupid for not getting vaccinated, or mocking them for asking reasonable questions about side-effects, won't convince them to have a jab. Instead, they need to be given every opportunity to put any questions to a trusted, knowledgeable person from their own community, preferably a medical professional, who can hopefully put their minds at rest. This can then lead to an effect called self-persuasion where a person's attitude is changed from the inside rather than the outside, as it were. And, indeed, it is through this 'softer' and more understanding approach that vaccine hesitancy among sections of the population has been successfully reduced to some extent.

But hang on, I've noticed – and you may have too – that in the last paragraph I've moved in a rather slippery way from the respectful and neutral position of trying to under-stand an anti-vaxxer's point of view to considering how, from their perspective, they might come to agree with me. This slipperiness illustrates how difficult it is to genuinely empa-thise with someone you disagree with, for however much you try to see things their way, you are always tipping back towards your own viewpoint. In this case, willing the anti-vaxxer to come over to the pro-vaccination side, which, it could be argued, is not really empathy at all, but rather a subtle form of coercion.

There is also another problem that can stem from putting yourself in the mind of a person whose views diverge from yours. As psychologist Zak Tormala found from an experiment at Stanford University, sometimes trying to understand things from the perspective of someone with a different world-view from you can actually lead you to become even *more* entrenched in your own view and – worse still – *harden* your dislike of the person who disagrees with you.[7]

Tormala and his team recruited a number of people to take part in his experiment, all of whom expressed an interest in politics. Some were on the Left and some were on the Right. They were told that they would be generating arguments concerning the Universal Basic Income. This is the idea that every citizen of a state is paid, by right and for life, a sum of money sufficient to live on, in addition to any other income they might earn. The participants had been asked what their own view of this policy was. Then they were asked to imagine a person who held the opposing view to them. One group was told that this person also held different political opinions from them more generally, while a second group was told that the person held similar general views to them and just happened to disagree on this issue. Both groups were asked to spend some time imagining what the person's life was like, the experiences they had had, and what interests and motivations they might have. Then they had to think of an argument that this person might give that countered their personal view of the basic income.

And bear with me, because there was a third group too. This control group didn't imagine a particular person, and simply had to come up with an argument about the basic income counter to their own view.

The results surprised even Zak Tormala (although he's generous enough to admit that his doctoral student predicted this all along). The people who softened their own attitudes the most were those who imagined what it was like to be the person who disagreed on this one issue but held similar political views in general. When the person held a different ideology in general, trying to empathise with them backfired; they became even less receptive to their opposing view on the issue at hand than the people in the third group, who hadn't even tried to put themselves in another person's shoes. So, in terms of trying to understand people it would have been better not to try to see things from the other's perspective.

The conclusion from this study might be seen this way: it's easier to step into another person's shoes, however poorly the shoes fit, if you like the rest of a person's outfit. This tendency is known as 'value congruence' and it explains why in so many ways human beings are tribal and why so-called 'culture wars' can be so toxic. The point here is that what often divides us is not our views on specific issues, whether it be the Basic Income or being vaccinated against Covid-19 but rather a broader sweep of opinion, a 'world-view', which takes in political sympathies, positions on social and ethical issues, and what the US founding fathers called 'self-evident truths'. For all I know there are many things on which I and, say, David Attenborough, disagree. But I have a feeling that in the wider sense, we are on the same 'side'. I'd therefore cut him much more slack on points of divergence between us than I would with, say, Donald Trump.

This suggests we might need to be wary of using perspective-taking as a technique when the ideological gulf between ourselves and others is wide. In these situations, considering how the other person might justify their stance on a particular issue could reinforce our own divergent view on this issue and a wide range of other issues. As a result of the perspective-taking in these cases, we become more convinced we have nothing in common and our sense of distance from, and distaste for, that person only increases.

The great daff robbery

I used to live in a flat with a not very attractive front door, in an alleyway that was often full of piles of old cardboard boxes, put out by the owners of the shop below. In an attempt to make the entrance to our home look a little more welcoming, I bought two square grey planters to stand either side of the front door. Worried that the planters might get stolen, I fixed them to the path with concrete. In the autumn I planted daffodil bulbs and the following spring, when they bloomed, they really cheered up the alleyway, not just for me and my husband, and our downstairs neighbours, but for passers-by.

Then one morning, when I was locking up on my way out, I realised something looked different about the entrance to our building. Every single daffodil flower and stem in the planters had been cut off – and it had clearly been done neatly with scissors. This wasn't drunk students on their way back from the pub who'd picked daffodils to put in each other's hair. This was a premeditated act of flower theft. I was furious. Each time I went in and out of the door in the days after, I saw the green stumps and was reminded of the meanness of the person who had stolen daffodils that I had taken six months to grow. It annoyed me so much that I had to find another way of thinking about it. I had to reframe it. So, I wondered, what reasonable circumstances might there have been for stealing the daffodils?

Back in the 1950s, a Chicago psychologist called Lawrence Kohlberg developed a model of six stages of moral development. To test it out he would give groups of boys a series of moral dilemmas. Here's an example of the kind of story he gave them:

A man called Heinz can't afford $1000 for the drug that could save his dying wife's life. He knows he is being overcharged for the drug by the chemist, he has been refused the opportunity to pay in instalments and he can't find anyone to lend him the money. Should he break into the chemist to steal the drug?

The answers the boys gave weren't important. What mattered was their reasoning. Typically, young children give possible imprisonment as a reason for not attempting the break-in, while others might suggest that Heinz goes ahead because he's unlikely to get caught. In both cases, the children's reasoning is basic: it's simple punishment and reward that matters most in their thinking.

But by the time the boys were about the age of 12, most of them were reaching higher stages in their moral development. They were beginning to consider the importance in our society of behaving in a way that gains approval from others and later, that laws should be obeyed because without them society would not function.

The sixth stage of reasoning, which not everyone reaches (although Kohlberg himself had, of course) is based on more complex ethical principles. Here a person sees that some laws are better than others and that sometimes it's OK to break the law if the system is unjust. In the Heinz dilemma, saving a life might be considered a higher principle than not stealing from a pharmacy.

All very interesting, I'm sure you'll agree, but how can Kohlberg's work be applied to the theft of my daffs? What ethical reasoning could explain such an outrageous act? I settled on the idea that the 'thief' was on their way to visit their dying mother in hospital. They were planning to buy flowers on the way, but then realised their wallet had been stolen. Knowing how much their mother loved flowers and that this was in all probability their last visit, they reasoned that it would be morally justifiable to take my daffodils, even though stealing was generally wrong.

True, I couldn't easily explain why the person happened to have scissors with them, but perhaps they had been making their mother a handmade card beforehand and happened to still have the scissors in their pocket? Or perhaps they were going to trim their dying mother's hair? Of course, my imagined scenario was implausible – there was no hospital nearby and this was most unlikely to be the true explanation – but that was not what mattered. What did matter was that through imagining a compassionate reason for the injustice done to me I was made to feel better about the situation.

The story of my stolen daffodils was much in my mind when I read a weighty and superb book called *The Compassionate Mind* by Professor Paul Gilbert who I mentioned earlier.[8] In his book he describes detailed exercises that you can do at home to improve your own levels of compassion. He gives the example of a friend who promised to phone at a certain time, but didn't. You'd stayed in to wait for the call and so you're left feeling angry that your friend could treat you like this. They clearly don't care about you, you think. They're selfish and thoughtless. Maybe they were never very bothered about you. Maybe no one else is really bothered about you either. These feelings consume you and ruin your evening, leaving you feeling rejected, lonely and cross – a distressing combination.

Is this a situation that sounds familiar? I'm guessing we've all been there. What, though, can we do about it? What should we do to make ourselves feel better?

Gilbert suggests using the techniques of cognitive behavioural therapy, not to deny your right to feel upset and let down, but to consider the thoughts and feelings you have about this situation and whether there might be an alternative way of viewing it. Some people might do this naturally, for others it will feel rather strange, but by working your way through a series of steps, you can start to feel calmer again.[9]

First, consider the facts. Might you see the situation differently if you were in a different mood to start with? What reasons, other than not caring, might your friend have for not calling you? What evidence do you really have to support your negative view of your friend's behaviour? How will you feel about this event in three weeks or three months' time?

Next, consider what might help you to cope at this moment. What has helped you successfully in similar situations in the past? What might another friend say to you now to make you feel better?

Now, you may be wondering where taking a compassionate stance comes into this. That comes next.

Put yourself in the position of the friend. Maybe something else came up – something really important – that stopped them calling you. Or maybe they genuinely forgot to call. It was a mistake and we all forget things sometimes, don't we? Their behaviour on this one particular day might be no reflection of the way they view their friendship with you. Think of the good times you've had together. There will be more to come in the future.

None of this is easy, especially in the midst of feeling so upset, but hopefully, as a result of asking yourself all these questions, you start to gain some sense of perspective and you calm yourself down. It may be that your friend doesn't deserve to be treated with such understanding. But on the other hand, by giving them the benefit of the doubt and putting the best construction on their behaviour, you could be responding fairly. Either way, the chances are you'll feel better.

Of course, a friend not phoning or losing a few daffodils are fairly trivial incidents. Using this technique is much harder, and less likely to bring comfort, when the act of harm done to you or someone you love has permanent consequences. Yet even after something as serious as a murder, relatives of the victim sometimes demonstrate extraordinary levels of understanding for the killers.

Take, for example, Colin Parry. His 12-year-old son Tim was killed by an IRA bomb in Warrington in 1993. From the very beginning and throughout the years since, Colin and his wife Wendy have sought to reach out to the people behind the attack. In an interview with their local paper, the *Liverpool Echo*, in 2009, Colin explained why: 'We wanted no more families to suffer as we and so many others had suffered. We wanted peace and that gave a sense of purpose to our lives which would otherwise have been empty of anything but grief and anger and incomprehension.'

This determination led Colin and Wendy to set up the Tim Parry Johnathan Ball Peace Foundation, a UK organisation working with the victims and survivors of political violence. (Johnathan Ball was the other victim of the Warrington bombing.) Colin Parry has said that if the people who actually carried out the attack contacted him and apologised, he would try to forgive them. And in an attempt to understand the motivation behind the terrorist attack, Parry has met with Sinn Féin leaders Gerry Adams and the late Martin McGuinness. He has gone to extraordinary lengths to understand the perspective of people who have brought such pain into his life.

It's hard to know the precise impact of the Parrys' actions. But relative peace has come to Northern Ireland since 1993 and people there and on the British mainland no longer live in constant dread of terrorist attacks from the IRA or other paramilitary bodies. The Parrys are undoubtedly exceptionally kind people and by demonstrating such forgiveness and compassion they must have had some effect on the actions of others, perhaps helping to push the protagonists in Northern Ireland's conflict to the peace table.

David Canter, who we met briefly earlier in this chapter, studies psychopaths. He does so, somewhat counterintuitively, in a hunt for the secrets of human kindness. Like a neurologist who studies damaged brains to work out how healthy brains function, Canter believes that by looking for signs of kindness in people who might appear to demonstrate a complete absence of this quality, he will get a better grip on how kindness works in the rest of us.

An intriguing finding from Canter's research is that people who score high on a kindness scale can also score high on an unkindness scale. This points to something we know from life: that human beings, ourselves included, are capable of being very kind at some times and most unkind at others. Remembering that fact alone can sometimes be helpful. So, the next time someone is horrible to you, try to react by thinking, 'this person is probably very nice in other circumstances'. It may not be easy to do, but it might make you feel better – and, more importantly, it's likely to be true.

Becoming more empathic

Because it's hard to empathise, but so important that we do so, we need to start thinking about empathy as a skill we can learn and get better at, like cooking or driving. We need to realise that our ability to empathise with others, including those from other groups or people we disagree with, isn't innate and immovable. Rather, the more we work at being empathic, the more empathic we can become.

Carol Dweck, another Stanford professor, is known for her work on children's mindsets. She has demonstrated that children who believe – and are told – that they are very clever often stop pushing themselves, while children who haven't been doing so well at school start thinking they'll never do better. To overcome these problems, Dweck advocates teaching all children that intelligence isn't fixed, that you can move up – or down – in your attainment level, depending on the effort you put in and the risks you take.

So, could the same be true of empathy? Dweck and her

colleague, the social neuroscientist Jamil Zaki, thought so and carried out an experiment to find out.

They started by recruiting two groups of people, who were alike in their starting levels of empathy, but some of them believed that a person could become more empathic and some thought that wasn't true. Each group was then given a different magazine article to read about a woman called Mary. Both articles said that at school Mary hadn't been a very nice person, and in the article which the first group read, she now worked as a mortgage lender, sometimes repossessing people's homes when they hit hard times. The implication was that her level of empathy had remained low. Meanwhile, the second group read that as an adult Mary was active in her community, had become a social worker and cared very much about other people. The lesson of this version of the article was that we can all change, that empathy is a skill that can be acquired and we can become more empathic over time. What the researchers wanted to know was what influence these different lessons would have on the people in the two groups in terms of them showing empathy?

To measure this, both groups were asked how much effort they would put into supporting a cancer awareness campaign. The results showed the group who'd read about 'Mary the mortgage broker' was prepared to take part in arms-length activities such as sponsored runs. They didn't simply ignore the plight of cancer sufferers. But the group who'd read about the Mary who'd changed went further, pledging many more volunteer hours to activities that involved showing active empathy with cancer sufferers, such as sitting in on a cancer support group or hearing sufferers relate their painful stories.[10] The conclusion that Dweck and Zaki drew was that reading about just one person who has become more empathic can influence us to follow their example. The key point is that we don't have predetermined levels of empathy, we can learn or be inspired to be more actively empathic.

The good news is that there's evidence suggesting that what you'd hope to be true is true: that more empathy leads to more kind actions. Indeed in the Kindness Test there is a strong relationship between people's empathy and their levels of kindness.

Let me tell you about Katie Banks. It's a very sad story. She was at university when her life was upended by a shocking car accident. Both her parents and one of her sisters were killed in the crash, leaving Katie, another sister and their brother as orphans. These siblings were both teenagers and were still at school, so Katie needed to care for them. This meant she had little time for her university work. But if she didn't study, she wouldn't pass her final exams and wouldn't be able to get a good job to support her family. She was faced with a seemingly insoluble dilemma, one she feared might end with her siblings having to be adopted by someone else.

I should say at this point that Katie's story is fictional (although while writing this chapter I did read a magazine feature by a woman who went through an uncannily similar experience and, happily, made it through her final exams). The Katie story was created by the American social psychologist Daniel Batson and he did so in order to measure the extent to which it's possible to induce empathy in a person and make them act in a kinder way.[11]

Over three decades Batson has conducted numerous experiments and, partly because he often uses radio interviews, I really like his methods. In the Katie Banks case, he asked volunteers to come into the lab and then he played them an interview with her on cassette. (This, I should explain, was not some sort of retro experiment, using cassettes because they're cool. No, these experiments began in the 1980s, when cassettes were still current technology.) Anyway, the people taking part were given varying instructions on how they should listen to the interview with Katie. Some were told to be as objective as possible about what had happened to her and not to get caught up in how she felt. Others were told the opposite and were asked to imagine Katie's emotions and how her life had been affected. And a third group were asked not to concentrate on how Katie felt, but on how *they* would feel if this tragedy had happened to them. Afterwards everyone was asked what level of support they thought Katie needed.

Not surprisingly, everyone thought she was in need to some extent. And it's probably not a surprise either that the people who were told to imagine how Katie felt or how they'd feel in her place, showed more empathy towards her plight than those who were told to remain aloof and objective. But there was another distinct difference between the three groups – and this is perhaps less predictable. Those who imagined the accident and its aftermath had happened to them also felt more distressed than those who'd imagined what it felt like for Katie.

Here then is an example of where putting yourself in someone else's shoes can be a good thing – if, that is, it leads to enhanced empathy levels. People are sometimes criticised for acting kindly if they do so in order to relieve their own distress. This tendency is known as egoistic motivation and is not generally seen as an attractive quality. But if the result is that people who need kindness receive it, what's the problem? To take one example, if you give money to a disaster relief appeal mainly because you can't bear to see the upsetting scenes on television it is surely better than not donating at all?

Batson rarely uses the word 'kindness' in his work, but reading his research it seems clear to me that his experiments do demonstrate that we are fundamentally disposed to be kind to others. His work displays, as he himself says, with 'remarkable consistency' that people lean towards acting in a kindly way.[12] Again and again he shows that people help, share with and give more to people for whom they feel empathy. He has found that if you ask people to imagine life from another person's perspective, they're more likely to help even if the help is anonymous and so there's no public credit to be gained. He's shown that even if there's an easy way to avoid helping, even if it's easy enough to justify failing to help, and even when not helping would be more fun, people still help others. And more than that, once people have felt empathy for someone they will even help after that person lets them down. You can set up a game on a computer where people can choose whether to cooperate with another player, or to treat them unfairly. Remarkably, once people have started to empathise with the player, they will often carry on helping them, even when they know for certain that the other player has already let them down.[13] Once we feel empathy for someone, it seems that sometimes we just can't help but be kind.

Maybe we shouldn't be surprised that we can, in myriad ways, be induced to empathise with others. After all it's what novels and films have been doing for years. They show that you don't have to know or meet, say, a boy born in a workhouse, orphaned, apprenticed to an undertaker and tricked into joining a gang of pickpockets, to understand the plight of Oliver Twist. In fact, you can imagine the situations he finds himself in, feel sorry for him and put yourself in his place. It doesn't even have to be a human being. After all, who doesn't feel great empathy for the plight of a marmalade-loving bear from Peru in the *Paddington* stories? Or who doesn't identify with the cheeky little steam train, Thomas the Tank Engine, and feel for him when Gordon, the bigger locomotive, teaches him a lesson? In 2021 there was even a series of experiments published which showed it was possible to induce empathy in human beings for our oceans, as a way of getting us to care for the marine environment better. Half the people were put in a virtual reality scene where they were standing on the deck of a fishing trawler, while a voiceover described a dystopian future where authoritarian governments are on the rise, there's little support for sustainability and illegal fishing is increasingly prevalent. Then they find themselves under the water with hundreds of fish swirling around them, and by the time the narrator has finished telling them that deep sea habitats have been damaged and poverty levels have soared, the number of fish swimming around them has dwindled, until eventually there's just an empty blackness in the ocean.[14] The other half of the people were immersed in a more optimistic scenario where action was taking place and fishing stocks recovered. It probably won't surprise you to learn that the people who watched the pessimistic scenario developed the most empathy for the oceans. But what's intriguing for me is that our empathy can be extended far beyond humans to our oceans and the wider world.

When there's a corresponding change in attitude it's known in psychology as the empathy-attitude effect. Its power can perhaps be best demonstrated when it is applied to our feelings towards people who we have most reason to dislike, such as convicted murderers and drug dealers, say.[15] In 2002, Daniel Batson played to volunteers the tape of an interview with a very different figure from Katie Banks. This time the interviewee was a 22-year-old man called Jared, who was in the second year of a seven-year sentence for using and selling heroin – not on the face of it a character with whom people were likely to empathise. But once the volunteers had listened to Jared's hopes and fears for the future, made a connection beyond his criminality, and started to see things from his perspective, they not only felt more concern for him, but they acted on it. More strikingly, they also wanted to help other drug users whose stories they hadn't heard, and when they were given the opportunity to vote for more funds to go to a drug outreach programme at the expense of other charities, including an environmental organisation and an educational charity, they did so.[16]

So far in this section we've seen that it is possible to induce empathy during a quick experiment in lab. But what about something longer lasting?

Paul Gilbert has shown that it's possible to train people to feel more compassion using techniques related to meditation. I've summarised one of his exercises below. It doesn't take long to do and there are many more examples like this that you can try.

- Stand loosely and breathe in a relaxed rhythm for roughly 30 seconds.
- Start to imagine that you are a deeply compassionate and wise person.
- Think what ideal qualities you would like to have as that person. (Whether you have those qualities already doesn't matter; you are thinking about your desire to have them.)
- Imagine the compassionate facial expressions you'd make if you were this sort of person.
- All the while, feel your body relaxing.

Gilbert says you can practise this simple technique any time of day and wherever you happen to be. You should always remember that you are in training so don't feel under pressure to achieve quick results.

You can also practise having kind thoughts about other people, imagining your friends and your desire for them to be happy, and then widening it to people you know less well.

Mental exercises like these take time to master and can at first feel uncomfortable or strange. But eventually, most people feel at ease doing them. And the results can be impressive. Gilbert's research shows that after several weeks people report having nicer feelings about other people, while also feeling better about themselves. Sometimes these techniques are referred to as loving kindness meditation or compassion meditation or compassion training. Exact methods vary, but the idea is the same: to develop our long-term sense of compassion.

Importantly, this training not only makes us *feel* more compassionate towards others, but also translates into an increased level of kind *actions*. For example, Tania Singer from the Max Planck Institute in Leipzig gave people compassion training and found that when they were given computer games to play afterwards, they were more likely than those who hadn't had the training to help strangers who were playing in the games.[17]

In another study, Singer first asked a group of volunteers to do some basic empathy exercises in which they were taught to try to empathise with the suffering they witnessed. Then during a brain scan they watched short film excerpts from news programmes and documentaries in which people sustained injuries or lived through natural disasters. The participants were asked how they felt and their neural responses were compared. Those who'd had simple empathy training were more likely than the control group to show activation in the areas associated with experiencing pain – it was as if they themselves were suffering the pain they witnessed. But up to this point, the study didn't advance on research we've seen elsewhere in this chapter.

The difference came when the same group were then given more intensive compassion training which taught them to extend caring feelings to the people who they saw suffering. When, after this training, they were again shown videos of people suffering, their brain responses differed from before, this time displaying activation in areas of the brain associated with love and reward, suggesting a stronger empathic reaction. They also reported feeling differently. After empathy training, watching suffering made them feel bad, but after compassion training, they felt more positive.[18]

It's a striking finding suggesting that after undergoing the more advanced form of training people not only feel more empathic towards those who are suffering, but more energised to do something to relieve that suffering.

The ins and outs of empathy

This doesn't mean more empathy in every situation is always better. There are situations where if we feel another person's pain too strongly the intensity can overwhelm and even paralyse us, leaving us unable to act as kindly as we could. In the next chapter I'll be looking at an extreme type of kindness – heroism. If you are faced with someone flailing about in the water after they've fallen into a canal it perhaps isn't that helpful if your main reaction is to imagine you yourself are drowning. That could lead you to stay on the towpath doing nothing when you might have been able to rescue the person.

When he was writing a book on empathy, Paul Bloom often noticed that people were very approving of his subject matter, assuming he'd think empathy was wholly good. They were taken aback, therefore, when he told them the title of his book – *Against Empathy*.[19] Of course, Bloom isn't against *all* empathy, just what he sees as the excessive sort, which he argues can skew good judgement. One example of this is the identifiable victim effect whereby all the focus is put on the people who featured in the news item or charity campaign (remember Pete from Chapter 3 and the 90 glasses of red wine he was given), sometimes at the expense of others in a similar plight or other, perhaps more important, issues.

Bloom asks us to imagine a girl with a terminal disease who is on a waiting list for treatment to ease her pain and maybe even help her live longer. The more we learn about the girl, the more empathy we feel for her, and the more likely any of us would be to want her pushed to the top of the waiting list. But that would come at the expense of other children, also suffering pain and facing death, whose names we don't know. And maybe by focusing on one little girl's plight we are diverted from bigger issues – a lack of investment in health services or a shortage of specialist doctors.

The effective altruism movement tries to counter the temptation to give to the causes that might appeal to us personally, by trying to work out how funds can have the greatest impact, often using statistical analysis to guide the decisions to give. This has benefitted, for example, charities distributing bed nets to prevent the spread of malaria in sub-Saharan Africa, where a life can be saved for a smaller sum than in a richer country. Of course the outcomes will only be as good as the metrics used and there is a risk of removing the feel-good factor that encourages so many of us to give. Then again there are still plenty of people giving to the causes that have affected their families or friends, so we end up with a mixed economy, which might seem messy, but could be a good way through.

Another example of how kindness can go awry is illustrated by the still fairly common practice of giving work experience to a friend's child. It might seem kind to respond positively to such a request, but the price is paid by young people who aren't as well connected and who lose out in the jobs market. In situations like these, we need to ask ourselves if our kindness is fairly distributed. Is it really a kind act to say yes?

Certainly, decades of psychological research on discrimination against outgroups has demonstrated that inequity is not only caused by deliberate actions, but by members of ingroups favouring their own. So, if I do help the daughter of a friend of mine by agreeing that she can 'shadow' me in my work, I am – without meaning to or wanting to – privileging this young woman over a young woman I don't know, who might be in a more disadvantaged situation and more in need of my help.

Back in the 1970s the social psychologist Henri Tajfel conducted experiments, now considered classic studies, on what he called 'minimal groups'. From these experiments, he developed the concept of social categorisation which explains our cognitive process for simply and quickly sorting people into groups. So, if you are meeting someone called Frank off a train and you don't know what he looks like, but you do know that he's a teacher, rather than ask every single man if they're Frank, you'll look for men you think look like a teacher, based on what they're wearing or carrying. Are they, perhaps, wearing a corduroy jacket with leather elbow patches and carrying a suitcase stuffed with exercise books? (I'll admit my image of teachers may be a bit out of date these days.)

You might get your categorisation wrong, of course, but experience – and evidence – shows that you'll often be right – and the process saves a lot of time and bother. In this way then, the mental shortcut provided by social categorisation is useful and justifiable. But it becomes a real problem when we start to stereotype people negatively. We can all think of obvious examples of this problem, perhaps most notoriously the tendency to see young Black men wearing hoodies as a threat or women wearing head coverings as victims of male oppression.

Obviously, the most significant ingroups and outgroups develop over years, decades or even centuries, based on social bonds, geography, nationality and ethnicity. But Tajfel's work showed that a minimal group – displaying ingroup and outgroup tendencies – can be established very quickly. In fact, a single toss of a coin can be enough to lead us to take 'sides' and demonstrate loyalty to our own side and even antagonism towards the other side.

In tests, the tasks Tajfel gave different groups to perform were in themselves simple. One involved the participants having to learn a list of words and then repeat them from memory. Stumbling or taking a long time to remember a word led to a participant getting a loud, unpleasant noise blasted through their headphones, while doing well was rewarded with sweets or small cash prizes. It might all seem rather inconsequential, but the findings from the study were striking because again and again members of Group A were relatively fair, but slightly more generous towards other members of Group A than they were towards Group B – and vice versa. It became clear that even though people were randomly assigned to their group, they had no prior relationships or bonds, and there was no group identity beyond the games being played, group members slightly favoured their 'own' over the 'other'. (Indeed, so strong is this tendency within us all that other experiments have shown that children as young as three react in the same way.) The only silver lining in Tajfel's studies was that although people gave their own group more than their fair share of sweets, they only gave a few more unpleasant noises to the other group than to their own. In other words, they showed more favouritism than discrimination. Though of course the result can be much the same. If white people give all the jobs to other white people rather than people of colour, it's not much of a defence to say this is 'looking after your own'.

And if you remember, what's worrying is that even random membership of a group based on the toss of a coin is enough to trigger strong 'in' and 'out' group effects.[20]

In fact, if it wasn't sometimes so serious, our propensity to form minimal groups based on pretty much anything would be laughable. For instance, it's been demonstrated that we like people with the same birthday as us better than people with other birthdays. And one study found that our attachment to the first letter of our names is such that we're more likely than by chance to do a job that begins with the same first letter as our name. Yes, you read that right. In the study the researchers looked at roofers and hardware store owners and found that a Rex was more likely to become a roofer than a hardware shop owner, while in a Harry's case it was the opposite – and that this propensity was so marked it was statistically significant.

I always like it when academics submit papers to serious journals with jokey titles and all these examples come from an article called 'Why Susie Sells Seashells by the Seashore'.[21] So a Susie is more likely than a Maisie to open a shell shop at the seaside while Maisie (I'm guessing) is more likely to make maple syrup in Maine. I could go on. For instance, the same authors looked at every woman who had a baby in Texas in 1926 (as you do) and found that this cohort of women were 40% more likely than by chance to have married a man with a surname that had the same first letter as that of their maiden name. The same was true, more or less, in Georgia, Florida and California. Moreover, a statistically disproportionate number of people named Virginia moved to the state of Virginia, while people called Louis or Louise were more likely to move to Louisiana.

Before you try to find a way of setting your dating app to offer only matches with the same initials as you, I should add that there's been some questioning of the methodologies used in some of these studies and one critical analysis found the first-letter-of-name effect only applied to the brands that people like best.[22] They don't give examples alas, but I'm assuming that Vicky flies Virgin and Emily prefers Emirates.

But even so, the overall evidence points in the same direction: we can identify with others and form quite strong groups based on insignificant and flimsy associations. So when we are considering how we distribute our kindness, we might want to ask ourselves which groups of people we are favouring and why.

Switching off empathy

Perhaps you know the game Operation? In it, players use a little pair of tweezers to try to remove objects from a plastic, pot-bellied man (his pot belly cleverly hides his genitals incidentally, or maybe the lack of them) without touching the sides of his open 'wounds'. There's no hiding place for clumsy 'surgeons' because if the 'scalpel' does slip, there's a buzz and the man's nose lights up. I used to like this game even though I wasn't very skilled at it, finding it impossible to control my nerves and keep my hand steady as I attempted to extract the plastic bread basket from the man's tummy or the Adam's apple from his throat or the butterfly from his stomach. It was almost as if I feared causing real pain to the poor pink patient with his constantly flashing honker.

Real surgeons have to overcome any squeamishness they feel during operations or they wouldn't last long in the profession. Of course, these days anaesthetics help the patient, but also the doctor, who generally isn't inflicting actual pain during surgery. However, there are procedures that require patients to be awake and these can sometimes be 'a little uncomfortable', which tends to be a medical euphemism for 'bloody agony'.

Medical staff learn to cope with the sights – and sounds – of others in pain by cutting themselves off emotionally and not seeing things from the patient's perspective. I've been out by helicopter to critical incidents and the emergency air ambulance teams behave utterly professionally, but simply can't afford to spend time comforting people at the scene of an accident. They need to act, not empathise. Research shows that their brains even begin to respond differently to witnessing pain. For instance, a study in Taiwan found that if you get a non-doctor to watch a needle being inserted into another person's arm, one part of the brain is activated, a part associated with responding to the infliction of pain. If, on the other hand, that non-doctor sees a cotton bud being pressed against the arm, there's a different brain response. In a doctor however, there is no difference in the brain's reaction to these two different cases. The doctor's brain is, in effect, screening him or her from the normal response to witnessing pain.[23] Of course, on occasion, the price they might pay – or rather, we might pay – is to underestimate a patient's pain, sometimes with serious results, but on balance the benefits outweigh the disadvantages.

Indeed, this closing down of empathy can help doctors to do more than just cope with the emotional strain of their work; it might actually assist them in honing their skills. This was demonstrated in a study by Lasana Harris, a psychologist at University College London. He took a group of people who weren't doctors and gave them each an arm made of rubber. He then asked his volunteers to do some stitching on the arms, as if they were sewing up a wound. Now, rubber arms they may have been, but they were very realistic and some of the volunteers found the exercise difficult because they could imagine the pain they'd be causing if these were actual arms. As a result, those who scored highest on empathy were much worse at stitching, while those with lower empathy levels were better at it (surgeons in the making perhaps?).[24]

In October 2021 I interviewed Brett Campbell, an intensive care doctor working in Nashville, Tennessee, who by then had been treating patients with Covid-19 for more than 18 months. He thought he'd seen the worst of the pandemic in the first few months of 2021, but then the Delta variant came along. The patients coming into ICU with Delta were younger. And there was something else; they were less likely than previous patients to believe in the very existence of the disease that had made them so ill.[25]

'Certainly, a lot more people have been antagonistic towards the staff,' Dr Campbell told me. 'The unvaccinated population, probably in the country, but certainly in our area, seems to have a very different mindset about what the disease is, and what the risks are. They live in an environment or an echo chamber where it's believed that Covid is overblown, and so if they get sick, they seem to chalk that up to something besides the virus. I've had people come in and accuse the medical staff, people they've never met before, of being responsible for them getting sick, like, "You guys did this to me."

'There have been a few people who have refused to believe that they have had Covid when they've been admitted. No matter how much you tell them how sick they are or even that they are dying of Covid they have said, "No, I'm not, that's not what this is, you're lying".'

Dr Campbell finds he can put himself in the shoes of patients who didn't get vaccinated but are regretful once they've been hospitalised. But he tells me he has given up trying to understand those who accuse him of having made them ill, who still refuse vaccinations and deny that they have Covid. He knows it's his job to give them the best care possible and to try to save their lives, but he doesn't even attempt to empathise with these patients. He and his colleagues need to protect themselves from compassion fatigue and burnout, and even with people who are dying, they have found that shutting down like this is the only way to do that.

The 36 questions

Let's change tack for a moment.

Which famous person would you most like to have dinner with?

What does friendship mean to you?

OK, that's two questions not 36, but this is already quite a long chapter so I hope a flavour will do. You perhaps recognise the questions because they come from a famous list sometimes referred to as 'The 36 questions to fall in love'. Supposedly, by answering them you open up to a potential partner and thereby become closer to them and eventually – well, sometimes – you think 'this is the one!'

The academic name for the list is the Fast Friends procedure, which lacks a certain romance, though it was developed by a married couple, Elaine and Arthur Aron, both psychologists, who've spent half a century researching relationships together, which is a real tribute to their own compatibility.[26]

The idea is to recreate that 'talking-to-a-stranger-on-a-plane' experience, when strangers who just happen to have been seated next to each other end up having surprisingly deep and personal conversations. This happened to me once. I was on my own on a plane to France, reading a book about transhumanism in preparation for an interview I was doing. The Norwegian woman sitting next to me asked me what transhumanism was and we spent the rest of the flight discussing what we thought happened to us after death, and why some people go to great lengths to try to live on after their deaths through cryogenics or attempting to download their brains onto hard drives. We continued the conversation while we queued at passport control and waited at the luggage carousel. After such a profound personal conversation devoid of small talk, it felt slightly odd saying goodbye and walking away, never to see each other again, when our respective friends, leaning on the barriers waiting, waved to us.

The Fast Friends procedure takes things a little more slowly. Two people sit down together and discuss their answers to the questions, starting with the famous dinner guest question and very, very gradually getting deeper and more personal until they get to questions about what they most regret about their upbringing, or to number 35 on the list which is: 'Of all the people in your family, whose death would you find most disturbing? Why?'

This set of questions was developed in 1997 and is still being used in academic research to this day, including in studies designed to reduce suspicion and hostility between different ethnic groups.[27] The results can be impressive with clear findings that prompting dialogue in this structured way can lead to a decrease in people's anxiety about interacting with different ethnic groups.[28]

New research also appears to confirm that people quite like having a deep conversation with a stranger and definitely more than they expect to. In this recent study, volunteers in the lab were given topics to discuss with someone they didn't know beforehand. Sometimes the topics were on the lighter side, such as TV programmes or hairstyles. But at other times, the topics were much deeper. Questions such as: 'Can you describe a time when you cried in front of someone else?' or 'For what in your life do you feel most grateful?'

When they first saw the list of questions, the participants in the study were nervous about the deeper topics. Surely it would be awkward discussing such things with a stranger, they thought. In fact, it turned out they felt happier after the deeper conversations and that these chats were a lot less awkward than they anticipated.[29]

But you don't need to talk about profound philosophical and existential questions to establish a bond with someone else. In this book I've talked a lot about research conducted at Sussex University and the academic leading the Sussex

Centre for Research on Kindness there is Gillian Sandstrom. She specialises in studying conversations with strangers and, rather surprisingly perhaps, her research shows that simply initiating a conversation with a stranger – it doesn't matter what you chat about; the weather will do – puts both parties in a measurably better mood.

In an experiment at Tate Modern in London, Gillian arranged for volunteers to start chatting with visitors about the exhibits. At first the volunteers were wary, wondering how their approaches would be received. After all, many people go to art galleries in search of peace and quiet, wanting to enjoy the artworks in silent contemplation, not to be drawn into conversation. But once the volunteers had been persuaded, not only did they enjoy the experience but the people to whom they chatted did too. They may have been guinea pigs of random 'chat-bombing' but they left the gallery saying they'd experienced an improvement in mood and felt more connected with other people.

It won't surprise you to learn that people who score high on extraversion and low on shyness are less nervous about starting conversations with strangers. But you might be more surprised to discover that although most of us think we're better than average at many things (a statistical impossibility known as the Lake Wobegon Effect), we don't tend to think this is true when it comes to striking up conversations, which may explain why we can be reticent about doing it. That is a shame, because although we are cautious about chatting with people we don't know, other studies by Gillian Sandstrom show the chances of being rebuffed are surprisingly rare.[30]

It's something to think about next time you're on a train:

179

who knows, maybe if you asked the person seated next to you: 'Do you have a secret hunch about how you will die?' – number seven of the 36 questions – they'd respond enthu-siastically rather than getting up and moving to the other end of the carriage muttering, 'Weirdo'.

But seriously, Gillian Sandstrom goes as far as to say that talking to strangers is an act of kindness and she's found that the conversations don't have to deal with life and death to have beneficial effects. Even seemingly shallow conversa-tions and tiny interactions highlight our connection with others and our shared humanity, reminding us that despite the polarisation we might see online or in politics, we do have something in common.

Like those volunteers in the Tate, our fear of course is that if we reach out to strangers we might be rebuffed. But using an app, Sandstrom has set people the task of having multiple conversations with strangers within a short time-frame and the results have so far been positive. Yet at the same time she persistently finds that many of us try to avoid conversations with strangers and some people, of course, dread them. Again, the problem seems to be that we worry that the other person won't enjoy the discussion and that they won't like us.[31] Both of these findings reveal people to be rather kind.

As I mentioned earlier, people who score high on extra-version and low on shyness are less nervous about initiating conversations with strangers. The Kindness Test provided more evidence that this was true. More strikingly, regardless of personality type, the people who tend to talk to people they don't know on average received more acts of kindness. And in addition, they observed more kind acts going on around them, which is important because it gives you a sense of living in a more positive, connected world.

I also wonder whether things are changing for the better in this regard. Many people have commented on how strangers were much more likely to smile and chat during the first Covid-19 lockdown, and one of the chief findings in the Kindness Test was that two thirds of people (in Britain at least) think the pandemic has made people kinder. Perhaps this is explained by the fact that, because of self-isolation and social distancing, we only had limited amounts of inter-action with other people, so we valued the human connections we were able to make.

It will be interesting to see if this trend continues now that restrictions on mixing and meeting have in many countries been removed. If some of us started talking to strangers more during the pandemic, maybe we won't be afraid to carry on.

Listen, truly listen; read, read seriously

In any conversation, whether it be with a stranger or a friend, the key to empathic kindness is to listen, truly listen. We tend to assume we're listening, but often we're not paying as much attention as we think. I know that goes for me, even when I'm interviewing people on my podcasts and radio shows. It's true that I am concentrating hard so that I don't make the mistake (easily done when there's lots to think about) of asking my guest a question they've already answered, but even so I'm not unconditionally listening because I can't. I'm watching the clock to check the timings are going to fit. I'm listening to the quality of the line, wondering if it's useable if the Wi-Fi drops out at some point. I'm listening to the producer suggesting extra questions in my ear or warning me that the time is nearly up.

By the same token, I'm sure many of the listeners to my shows believe they are paying full attention, but a lot of the time they are distracted by other things. Intense listening isn't easy.

Much of the time the fact that what other people say to us goes 'in one ear and out of the other' – and without touching the sides – is not perhaps very important. But there are times when it is essential to really try to listen. Kathryn Mannix, the author of a book called, appropriately, *Listen*,[32] has spent many years working in palliative care with people who are dying. She says if you want to have a particularly important conversation in your personal life, you should embark on it not in the spirit of 'a good talking to' but 'a good listening to'. For it is only through humble, generous, immersive listening that we can really understand another's perspective and act in a truly kind way.

There is, though, an alternative to deep listening; it is something I mentioned earlier – reading. The novelist Elif Shafak argues in her recent book *How to Stay Sane in an Age of Division* that too much of our reading these days is superficial and only involves us gleaning small snippets of information, some of it misinformation, from social media.[33] Her solution to this problem is for us to read more books, longer books, books the author has really invested time in.

Now, you might expect an acclaimed writer to argue this – she has a vested interest in people doing more serious reading, after all – but there is plenty of scientific evidence to back up Shafak's idea. Studies have shown reading fiction can result in everything from an increase in volunteering to our propensity to vote.[34] The secret power of novel reading is that it is like a training course in perspective-taking without us even noticing.

Aristotle said that when we watch a tragedy two emotions predominate – there is pity for the depicted character, along with fear for ourselves. We imagine what it's like to be, say, Antigone, and compare her reactions to the way we may have responded in the past or imagine we might in the future (though thankfully few of us will ever face being entombed alive in a cave). Keith Oatley, a cognitive psychologist based in Canada, calls fiction 'the mind's flight simulator'. Just as flight simulators allow pilots to feel what it is like to fly a plane, so novels allow us to feel what it is like to be another person. Oatley's research shows that when we start to identify with a character in a novel, we start to consider their goals and desires instead of our own.[35] His work has also shown that the more fiction and non-fiction people read the better they are in tests of interpersonal sensitivity and in detecting which emotion people are expressing with their eyes.[36]

Good reading requires the skill known as theory of mind, a skill which allows us to understand that others have their own views which are different from ours, and which in 'the real world' enables us to engage successfully in social inter-action. Studies have shown that when we read about how a character in a book feels, the areas of our brains associated with theory of mind are activated – even though we know that this character is made up.[37] More than that, when we read the word 'kick', areas of the brain related to physically kicking are activated, while if we read that a character pulled a light cord, activity increases in the region of the brain associated with grasping.[38]

What most interests me is whether the enhancement that we get from reading in understanding other people's emotions translates into kindness in practice. To test this, researchers have used a method many a psychology student has used at some point, where you 'accidentally' drop a bunch of biros on the floor and then see who offers to help you gather them up. In this particular study, before the pen-drop took place participants were given a mood questionnaire interspersed with questions measuring empathy. Then they read a short story and answered a series of questions about the extent to which they'd felt transported while reading the story. The experimenters then said they needed to fetch something from another room and, oops, dropped six pens on the way out. I'm pleased to say, the people who felt the most transported by the story and expressed the most empathy for the characters, were more likely to help retrieve the pens.[39]

It's possible, of course, that people who choose to read novels are already more empathic to start with. To account for this possibility with real accuracy, you'd want to start by measuring a group of people's empathy levels, then randomly allocate them either to read numerous novels or none at all, for years or even decades, and then only after this long period had elapsed measure their empathy levels again to see whether reading novels had made any difference. Not surprisingly, such a study has not been done. People may be happy to give a few hours or days to advance psychological understanding, but there are limits.

Instead, we have to rely on studies that look only at the short-term impact of reading on empathy levels. In one such study in 2013, Dutch researchers arranged for students to read either some newspaper articles about riots in Greece and Liberation Day in the Netherlands or the first chapter from the Portuguese Nobel Prize winner José Saramago's novel *Blindness*. In this story a man is waiting in his car at traffic lights when he suddenly goes blind. His passengers bring him home and a passer-by promises to drive his car home for him, but never arrives. Instead, he steals the car. When students read the story, not only did their empathy levels rise immediately afterwards, but provided they had felt emotionally transported by the story, a week later they scored higher on empathy than students who'd read the news articles.[40]

From this we can tentatively say that reading fiction might well encourage us to behave in a more kindly way. Certainly, some medical schools consider the effects of reading fiction to be so significant and beneficial that they now include modules on literature in their training programmes. This happens at the University of California Irvine's Department of Family Medicine, for example, and Johanna Shapiro from the department firmly believes that making medical students read serious fiction results in them becoming better – that is to say, more empathic – doctors.[41]

But to end this chapter I'm turning from fiction to fact, by sharing another entry from my Kindness Diary, an entry which illustrates perfectly how thinking from another's perspective can lead to a kind act.

Tuesday 7.10 p.m.
Came home from work to find that a tiny yellow watering can had been left on my front doorstep. Asked around. The immediate neighbours said it wasn't from them. So I think that a stranger with a watering can they no longer needed, spotting my little front garden full of flowers, saw things from my perspective and realised that since there are flowers in my front garden year round, I must use a watering can. And that I might like one. So they decided to leave it for me. Couldn't thank them, but it's the perfect size for my also very tiny greenhouse. When I use it I'll remember how kind they were. Might even make up for the stolen daffs.

LAST ACT OF KINDNESS
RECEIVED

The Kindness Test

My friend gave me a fossilised shark tooth.

Hillwalking, slipped & fell & hurt knees, someone helped me with aromatherapy oils, encouraged me to stay sitting & stopped me from feeling stupid!

My 11-year-old daughter wrote me a note telling me how much she loves me.

I got a nice compliment from a stranger.

I am isolated on a remote farm. I am a carer for my partner after a stroke. A friend and neighbour rings me every week to cheer me up.

I started crying at my beautician's about a personal matter and she comforted me with kind words and let me take my time. She was very warm and caring.

Someone shared a lovely video clip.

I bought a coffee. Then discovered I didn't have my wallet. She did not charge me for the coffee. Wallet handed in with nothing taken from it.

My wife found my glasses!

6

ANYONE CAN BE A HERO

'Some days you're the bug, some days you're the wind-shield.'[1] These are the words of Private Johnson Beharry, a now-famous British Army soldier, who was awarded the Victoria Cross – Britain's highest military honour – for saving two members of his unit from enemy ambushes in Iraq in 2004. Beharry insists he was just doing his job. He doesn't regard his feats of bravery as remarkable.[2]

I've not met Johnson Beharry, but I did meet another British Army hero, Lance Corporal Matthew Croucher. Croucher had less than seven seconds to decide whether to risk his own life in order to save his friends' after he set off a trip-wire booby trap while on patrol in Helmand Province in Afghanistan in 2008. 'I'd been through this scenario in my mind and realised there was nowhere to take cover. There's no point running off because you're going to catch shrapnel.'

So, Croucher dived onto the ground, rolled over and used his backpack to suppress the imminent blast. He was thrown into the air and landed some distance away. 'It took 30 seconds before I realised that I was definitely not dead.'[3] In fact, the only injuries he suffered were a nosebleed and perforated ear drums – which is astonishing when you see the state of his backpack, now on display at the Imperial War Museum in London.

From this incident, we can see that Croucher and his colleagues were saved by a combination of him knowing what to do in a given situation and remaining calm and collected enough to act on that knowledge. The bravery he showed came not from acting on pure instinct, but having the strength of mind to put his training into practice.

Matthew Croucher was later awarded the George Cross, but, like Johnson Beharry, he's remained modest about his actions, believing anyone faced with the same situation would have done the same.

Everyday heroes

Do you believe you could be a hero like Beharry and Croucher? I must say I have my doubts when it comes to myself. If I'm lucky I'm not going to find myself in a war situation. But there are circumstances where I might be called on to act bravely. Someone might fall from the platform at my local station, for instance. If that happened, would I be the person who jumps down onto the tracks to save them from the oncoming train? Or would I be one of the bystanders, watching on alarmed, yet inactive, while a perhaps preventable tragedy unfolded?

Evidence that I might, despite my doubts, turn out to be a hero in this situation can be found in a pocket green oasis squeezed into a crowded part of London between St Paul's Cathedral and the Museum of London. This is Postman's Park, so called because a large building at its southern end was once the home of the General Post Office, meaning the park was often used by postmen during their lunch break. The trim and tidy space, with its well-tended gardens, also sits next to the church of St Botolph's, Aldersgate, and like many of London's smaller parks, it's on the site of a former graveyard.

I visited the park on a chilly spring morning during the third UK Covid lockdown in March 2021, on one of the many long walks my husband and I went on at that time. The main reason for the visit was to see the park's most famous feature, the Watts Memorial to Heroic Self-Sacrifice. This consists of a wooden, cloister-like structure protecting 54 tablets, made of glazed ceramic tiles, fixed to the wall of what is now a block of flats. Each of the tablets briefly tells the story of an 'everyday hero', an ordinary person or group of people, who died trying to save the life of others.

There's a tablet honouring Sarah Smith, a young pantomime artiste, who died of terrible injuries at the Princes Theatre in London on 24th January 1863 when attempting to extinguish the flames that had enveloped a fellow dancer. And there's a tablet remembering Arthur Strange and Mark Tomlinson who tried to save two girls from drowning in quicksand in Lincolnshire but 'were themselves engulfed' on 25th August 1902.

Opened in July 1900, the memorial was the brainchild of the Victorian artist George Frederick Watts, and it shows, movingly and evocatively, that heroism is not the sole domain of soldiers and members of the emergency services, and that heroes are often otherwise ordinary, unremarkable civilians, of all ages, sexes and backgrounds. In his fascinating book on the Watts Memorial, the historian John Price also points out that 'everyday heroism' comes in different forms. He writes:

'The Watts Memorial has no shortage of . . . people running into burning buildings or jumping onto railway tracks . . . actions determined and driven by the urgency and jeopardy of the situation and characterised, to some extent, by the drama and spectacle that underpinned it.'[4] But alongside such acts there is also 'the heroism of careful and dedicated devotion, of professional commitment and responsibility, and of quiet, measured actions'. Such acts of heroism are, I believe, examples of perhaps the highest form of human kindness in which people sacrifice themselves for the sake of others, sometimes saving people they have never even met.

A poignant example of the latter, which has enormous resonance for all who've lived through the pandemic when so many health professionals put themselves in danger to save lives, is the story of William Lucas, a young doctor who performed an emergency tracheotomy on a child suffering with diphtheria. In the course of administering chloroform as an anaesthetic 'the child coughed or sneezed and his [Lucas's] face was peppered with infected mucus. Well aware of the dangers of infection in this manner, Lucas insisted on continuing with the operation rather than stopping to clean himself and the surgery was able to go ahead as planned.'[5] It's not known whether the child survived as a result of Lucas's brave and selfless professionalism, but Lucas himself died some weeks later, aged 23.

Along with Lucas, another young doctor is memorialised in Postman's Park – Samuel Rabbeth. In his case, knowing the dangers, he used his mouth to apply suction when a child's airway was blocked by the mucus caused by diphtheria. Like Lucas, Rabbeth was remembered in a number of ways, including in a poem published in the *Spectator*, which captures quiet, kindly heroism most beautifully:

No cry of battles rousing thy young blood,
urged thee to valorous deeds and hopes of fame.
Lowly to objectness thy loving task,
humble thy path, unknown 'til now thy name.[6]

Among the other acts of heroism commemorated by Watts are a number by children, including that of 11-year-old Solomon Galaman, who died from injuries he sustained while trying to save his younger brother from being run over on Commercial Street in Whitechapel. In a deathbed scene in the London Hospital that is almost Dickensian in its poignancy, little Solomon reportedly told his mother: 'Mother, I am dying. Have they brought my little brother home? I saved him, but I could not save myself.'[7] Other tablets record instances of young boys saving, or trying to save, not siblings, but friends – all instances of children acting in ways that belie the misplaced belief (which we explored in Chapter 1) that children are invariably selfish and unconcerned about the welfare of others.

Then there is a memorial to one of the most celebrated heroines of the Victorian age. Mary Rogers was a stewardess aboard the steamship *Stella*, which sailed regularly between Southampton and St Peter Port in Guernsey. On the 30th March 1899, when Mary was 44, the ship, which was on a special Easter excursion, sank after hitting the notorious Casquets rocks off Alderney. One hundred and ninety people were on board at the time and 86 passengers and 19 crew members died. Among those who gave up their lives was the captain of the ship – and indeed according to one survivor, a Miss Drake, 'the whole crew were heroes'.[8] But it was Mary who captured the public's imagination above all others, mainly through the testimony of another survivor, this time unnamed, which was published in the *Jersey Times* on 15th April, 1899.

> *Mrs Rogers, with great presence of mind and calmness, got all the ladies from her cabin to the side of the ship and after placing life belts on as many as were without them, she assisted them into the small boats. Then, turning around, she saw yet another young lady was without a belt, whereupon she insisted on placing her own belt upon her and led her to the fast-filling boat. The sailors called out, 'jump in, Mrs Rogers, jump in', the water being then but a few inches from the top of the boat. 'No, no!' she replied; 'if I get in, I will sink the boat. Good-bye, Good-bye' and then with uplifted hands she said, 'Lord, save me' and immediately the ship sank beneath her feet.[9]*

There are doubtless lashings of Victorian melodrama in this account, but it is first-hand testimony, and there is no doubt that Mary Rogers showed extraordinary calmness, kindness and self-sacrifice, saving many lives in so doing. As a result, she was widely venerated and there are memorials to her in Southampton, Liverpool and St Peter Port, as well as at Postman's Park.

Like the young doctors Lucas and Rabbeth, I doubt that Mary Rogers would have been comfortable with the label of hero or heroine. She would have considered that as a member of the crew of the *Stella*, she was only doing her job. But in her example, we see how devotion to duty can motivate people to exceptional selflessness. Another report of Mary's last moments has a passenger imploring her to get into a crowded lifeboat, but Mary replying, 'No, my place is here'.

The 'banality of heroism'

For a long time, psychologists have shown a lot more interest in our capacity for evil than good. But since the 1980s, interest in human goodness has grown. A prime example of this is the work of the psychologist Philip Zimbardo. Zimbardo is most famous, indeed notorious, for being behind the Stanford Prison Experiment in 1971, which appeared to demonstrate just how quickly ordinary people would begin treating people badly if they had power over them.[10] It's a study whose methods and findings have been frequently questioned and debated over the years.[11] It's clear that nothing about the experiment or the way it tends to be described is ever as straightforward as it sounds. However, Zimbardo isn't just interested in what drives us to act badly, he also wants to know what makes us behave well. This led him to set up the Heroic Imagination Project. The idea is to use psychological research to educate people on how they themselves could be a hero if the right moment presented itself. And it's certainly ambitious. In 2021, after ten years in which they trained 35,000 people in 12 countries, he said they were now 'moving from individual acts of heroism to building a critical mass to achieve collective heroism in order to shift the *hostile imagination* of our times into a more generic *heroic imagination*'.[12]

It's stirring stuff and, as if to demonstrate that while we can all be heroes only a special few are *super*heroes, it's accompanied by a big colour photograph of Professor Zimbardo, in which he is pictured wearing a Superman t-shirt, but with the S replaced by a Z. I've met and interviewed Zimbardo and he's a larger-than-life-character, so I'm not surprised to see the t-shirt. I have a photo of me with him in front of the San Francisco skyline in which he is also wearing a t-shirt with a picture of his own face on it. But regardless of the tops, he and his foundation are trying to do something significant, to save lives by encouraging each of us to realise that we could carry out a heroically kind act if necessary and this work has influenced the way I think about heroic acts of kindness. After years of research on heroism Zimbardo has concluded that, firstly, everyone is capable of heroic acts and heroism is certainly not the preserve of an elite minority. Secondly, people who do act bravely almost always seek to minimise their bravery afterwards, insisting they acted on instinct and that anyone would have done the same.[13] This apparent downplaying of everyday heroism – not least by the heroes themselves – led Zimbardo and his co-author Zeno Franco to coin the expression the 'banality of heroism', a conscious echo of the philosopher Hannah Arendt's term 'the banality of evil', which she used to explain how apparently normal people could perform monstrous acts during the Holocaust. (Her insights partly inspired the Stanford Prison Experiment, it should be noted.) Of course, this reworking of the expression could sound offensively dismissive if it wasn't for the fact that it chimes with the way many people labelled heroes like to see themselves: unremarkable, ordinary, typical. Ironically, perhaps, heroes more than anyone might embrace this coinage.

The rest of us though often remain resistant to 'it-was-nothing-really' claims, seeing them as examples of false or indeed heroic modesty, which only make us admire heroes even more. 'Not only are these people remarkably brave, they are remarkably self-effacing,' we say to ourselves, putting them on still higher pedestals and further distancing their actions from anything we can contemplate doing ourselves.

It's hard to study the personality traits of heroes, because they can only be identified as heroes *after* they've performed the heroic act, and we can't know that the experience itself hasn't somehow changed their personalities. We are left then with what we know about heroes *before* they became heroes, and that takes us back to the fact they come from all walks of life and in all shapes and sizes. It seems we keep being trapped inside the same conundrum: there is nothing obviously special about these special people until they perform their special act.

Still, when people were asked to list the personality traits they would associate with heroes, alongside the most popular words such as 'brave' and 'courageous' other words like 'caring', 'helpful' and 'compassionate' also appeared, all words which in the Kindness Test came within the top five words people gave to explain what kindness means to them.[14] This suggests that we see heroes as kind as well as daring – an important insight because, as a result, the field of heroism is opened up to a much wider range of people.

What remains to be explained is how this more widely shared capacity for selflessness converts into an actual act of heroism – or a failure to react heroically, as the case may be. A heroic act is in part dictated by the circumstances you find yourself in. So, the reason we can't believe we would jump into a canal to save a drowning child might be because we haven't been faced with that situation, rather than that we don't have it in us to act in such a way. Viewed this way, people become heroes not just because of what they did, but because they had the *opportunity* to do it.

Of course, this also means that our scope to demonstrate heroism is necessarily, indeed mercifully, limited. Or at least, that is true for the most striking forms of heroism, such as saving colleagues on the battlefield or pulling people out of burning buildings. This might be 'everyman' – and 'every-woman' and 'everychild' – heroism, in the sense that given the circumstances anyone might do it, but it is not 'everyday' heroism because we don't witness tragedies and accidents every day. Indeed, the renowned psychologists Bibb Latané and John Darley – whose work we will be looking at in more detail later on – estimated in a classic 1969 study that the average person will encounter fewer than six emergencies in a lifetime.[15]

But as I've already hinted, notions of what constitutes heroism have been broadening to include a greater range of human actions. Research on the Carnegie Medal for heroism in the US – which is presented to civilians – found that many more men had been awarded the medal than women, partly because so many categories involved acts of physical strength. But a broader definition of heroism includes plenty of women. In Chapter 3 we heard about Abie who donated his kidney to a stranger, but in fact kidney donors are more often women, who are making a sacrifice that demonstrates both kindness and bravery.

The classic definition of a hero might involve a great leader or warrior (usually a man) who shows bravery in service of his country. The psychologist Zeno Franco, who has divided heroism into three types, would put this type of hero – which includes Johnson Beharry and Matthew Croucher, but also historic figures like Napoleon or Alexander the Great, and the exceptional actions of firefighters and police officers – into his 'martial' category. But as I say, these days, and at least since the mid-nineteenth century, as Watts shows, we value two other types of hero just as much. Franco defines these categories as the 'civil' and 'social' – the first of these covering brave acts such as a civilian rescuing someone from a fire and a bystander intervening to stop a fight, while the second covers a number of areas, such as whistleblowing, being a good Samaritan, being an underdog who defies the odds and making scientific discoveries.[16]

If we accept these categories, we can easily see that the Postman's Park heroes largely conform to the 'civil' type. And in the next section, which looks at heroes of the pandemic, I go on to suggest a number of people and groups of people who I believe are good examples of 'social' heroes.

Pandemic heroes?

Early in the morning of New Year's Day 2020, Sarah Gilbert, a leading scientist at the University of Oxford, though still in her pyjamas, was up reading reports of a new 'viral pneumonia' in Wuhan in China. Perhaps the world can be thankful that Professor Gilbert wasn't, like many of the rest of us, enjoying a post-party lie-in, because this was the start of her team's development of a vaccine against what was soon to be known as Covid-19, in record time.

Since working on the 2014–16 Ebola outbreak, Professor Gilbert and her team at Oxford's Jenner Institute had engineered a generic vaccine which could be used as a building block for a more specific vaccine to tackle whatever deadly virus came along next. And they knew there was certain to be one. As she told my BBC colleague James Gallagher, 'We'd been planning for disease X, we'd been waiting for disease X, and I thought this (the Wuhan virus) could be it'.[17]

Professor Gilbert's work undoubtedly saved millions of lives and has helped life return to something much closer to normal than could ever have happened without vaccines. If that is not great work, work to be proud of, I don't know what is. But is it heroism?

I believe it is, and indeed it fits into Franco's 'social' hero category. Along with Sarah – now Dame Sarah – Gilbert, we might also include other virologists and epidemiologists and mathematical modellers who, while it's true to an extent that they were 'just doing their jobs', also went *beyond* the call of duty. It may have become irritating after a while to hear politicians talk about work to combat the pandemic going on 'tirelessly' and 'night and day', but in the case of Professor Gilbert and others, these statements were true. And while these scientists didn't put themselves in any danger as such – though the effects of burnout shouldn't be dismissed – they did show incredible humanity and selflessness, utilising every ounce of their skill and experience for the benefit of others.

And then there are the frontline health workers.

Over the 18 months or so that the pandemic was at its height, I interviewed numerous doctors, nurses and others working on the frontline for my podcasts. One of the most striking aspects of their accounts was that they were called on not just to perform medical tasks which, however harrowing, they all felt equipped to do, but also to show great kindness. With relatives and loved ones barred from hospitals and care homes for their own safety, it was left to doctors, nurses and support staff to provide patients with last words and touches of comfort. As well as administering drugs or performing medical procedures these professionals often found themselves giving hugs to fearful people in the final moments of their life.

When her mother was dying in hospital with Covid in England in March 2020 my best friend, Jo, was over 11,000 miles away in New Zealand, with no possibility of flying over to be at her mother's bedside. All my friend could do was to talk to her mum, Paula, online, and try to comfort her. A nurse, no doubt with many demands on her time, held the phone to Paula's ear and squeezed her hand while my friend spoke to her mum. By such means, the touch of a daughter was conveyed from the other side of the world to a dying mother. This act of kindness on the part of the nurse was a great consolation to Jo and hopefully to Paula too.

But the fact is that hugging dying people or facilitating deathbed conversations with relatives goes beyond what most nurses and doctors signed up for. Such actions don't come easily to all of these professionals, who as I've discussed in the previous chapter have learned to cope with the suffering and distress of their patients by keeping their distance from them personally, by deliberately not feeling too much empathy for them. It could therefore feel awkward, uncomfortable and even unnatural standing in, in some sense, for absent relatives.

And unlike the relatives who mostly faced loss only once, staff in hospitals and care homes were, during the worst of the pandemic, faced with repeated 'bereavement'. On some shifts, they would talk about life and death with a number of patients, only to find that when they came back to work the next day, several of those patients had died, while new people, who were equally sick, had taken their beds in the ward. Sometimes the last conversation they had with a patient was to ask them to consent to being put on a ventilator, explaining that if they didn't agree they were certain to die, but that if they did consent their chances were at the time only 50/50. All of this put staff at risk of what psychologists call moral injury, which happens when a person feels their response to a situation is inadequate, leaving them with feelings of guilt and shame.

This in part explained why some doctors and nurses objected to the regular Thursday evening 'clap for heroes', which took place during the first lockdown. They knew that all of us clapping and banging saucepans on our doorsteps meant well, but they didn't consider themselves heroes, but rather as people who weren't able to do their jobs properly because of inadequate protective equipment and a lack of intensive care beds.

It's also the case that being labelled a hero can hang heavy, which is why viewing such actions as acts of exceptional kindness, rather than heroism, could be helpful (and indeed kind in itself). In addition, such 'reframing' is another example of normalising heroism, putting it within reach of us, ordinary mortals, which in turn might mitigate some of the negative impacts of the so-called 'bystander effect', which I'll be exploring later in this chapter.

Before we leave the pandemic, let's also remember the late, great Captain Sir Tom Moore, who was another kind of 'social' hero during a time of crisis. He famously raised more than £30 million for NHS charities by walking 100 lengths up and down his garden before his 100th birthday. Sir Tom served in India and Burma in the Second World

War, and doubtless showed 'martial' bravery in action. But he was acknowledged as a hero, and rightly so, I believe, for undertaking an exceptional fundraising effort despite his great age and for showing such a warm, sunny and kindly disposition at a time when this was most needed.

One of the most important things about social heroes is that they serve as an active inspiration to others. Traditional forms of heroism can only happen when the situation arises and these cannot be manufactured – it is obviously less than heroic, for instance, to set your neighbour's house on fire so that you can then run into the flames to rescue them. But when it comes to exceptional philanthropy or perhaps starting a social movement (doesn't Greta Thunberg for instance qualify as a clear hero?) all of us, up to a point, can decide to follow in the footsteps of those who inspire us. We can become, as they say in HR, 'self-starters'.

This certainly happened in the case of Sir Tom, with numerous similar fundraising challenges being initiated. While the other older people who walked up and down their stairs ten times a day or went round the park daily in their wheelchair didn't achieve the worldwide recognition of the Captain, they did, in their own way, show as much heroism and compassion, and they in turn will have inspired others. Indeed, one of the great things about social heroism is that it can go viral, in the best sense of the word.

Standing down the bystander effect

But if it's true we can be inspired and encouraged to act as heroes, we can also sometimes be inhibited from doing the right thing. You've almost certainly heard of the 'bystander effect' which argues that the more people who are witnesses to a crime or an emergency, the less likely they are to inter- vene or help. This claim first emerged in a classic study by the psychologists John Darley and Bibb Latané in 1968 called 'Bystander intervention in emergencies'. Darley and Latané embarked on their research after hearing about the notorious case of Kitty Genovese in 1962 (which I mentioned in Chapter 1) when it was alleged – quite falsely, it later emerged – that 38 witnesses saw Kitty being stabbed, but did nothing. There's a problem with the bystander effect, though – and the problem is that it is nothing like as prevalent as is some- times claimed, as well as being hugely misunderstood.

Of course, if something bad happens in a crowd it is to a certain extent natural and certainly not irrational to assume someone else will react. You *could* confront the attacker, but then so could the person standing next to you, so why not leave it to them? Then there is the fact that in such a situa- tion, any blame that might stem from inaction is diffused among the group. OK, you didn't jump in and wrestle that gun off the robber, but then neither did anybody else. You can't be singled out.

You can in fact utilise this aspect of the bystander effect if you ever find yourself in need of assistance, by the way. Instead of just shouting 'Help, help' to the passing crowd, pick out just one person. 'You, there in the green jacket. Call the police! I need help!' If a specific person thinks the respon- sibility to intervene is theirs alone, there's a greater chance they will help you.

Another factor inhibiting intervention is the way society is constructed in some parts of the world these days, as we often lead individualised lives, cut off from our neighbours. How often, for instance, do you hear neighbours interviewed by journalists after a murder saying of the victims 'they kept themselves to themselves'? In such circumstances, it is perhaps hardly surprising that even if the opportunity arose, people would be reluctant to intervene to help other people they hardly know, particularly if by doing so they might well put themselves in extreme danger. We like to think we live in areas that are friendly and with a sense of community – the other thing you often hear people say to journalists after a murder is, 'I can't believe something like this happened around here' – but alongside a desire to be neighbourly and helpful to others, we are often held back by not wanting to interfere. And we've seen in the Kindness Test the chief reason people gave for not carrying out more kind acts is the fear that these acts would be misinterpreted.

And that embarrassment can be compounded by *us* fearing *we* might have misinterpreted the situation. In an emergency it's often not clear exactly what is happening, so it is common sense to hang back to assess what's happening, rather than rushing headlong into potential danger. We utilise a variety of cognitive processes to help us to decide whether or not to go to a person's aid – including, when there are others present, whether we are the best person to assist or how worried the other people seem. Our brains are working out the answers to such questions as whether that bloke over there is a stronger swimmer than we are and what you could throw to those kids or whether the rest of the crowd is right to assume they're just messing about in the water, having fun, rather than struggling to stay afloat. We don't want to get it wrong.

I've tried to imagine in the boxed section below how the

thought processes might differ between the hero and bystander when they see someone in danger at a railway station.

	Hero	Bystander
Observation of the incident	'Oh no! Someone has fallen off the platform and they're on the railway tracks.'	'Oh no! Someone has fallen off the platform and they're on the railway tracks.'
Assessment of what needs to happen	'Someone is going to have to jump down and help them. Perhaps it should be me?'	'Someone is going to have to jump down and help them. Surely there's someone other than me who'd be better at doing that?'
Assessment of whether to take action	'Someone has to act or the person could get run over by the next train. It could be dangerous, but I'm going to do it!'	'What will people think if I jump down? What if I've got the situation wrong? It could be dangerous. Thank goodness. Someone else has done it. Good for them!'
Explanation of personal actions afterwards	'Anyone would have done it. I just acted on instinct and did what needed to be done.'	'I am not like that hero. I don't think there are any circumstances in which I would act like them.'

Of course in an emergency these thought processes happen very quickly. And despite all the factors that could hold us back, like embarrassment and fear, heroes step forward. So what, if anything, makes them different? In a paper nicely entitled 'Are Psychopaths and Heroes Twigs off the Same Branch?' researchers discovered something striking about those who scored high on one particular feature of psychopathy known as 'fearless dominance' – which means they have a desire to dominate social situations, don't feel anxious about how their actions will look, are willing to take physical risks. So they might use their courage for ill, starting fights, say, but the researchers discovered that people with these characteristics were more likely than others to have carried out acts of heroism. Perhaps even more interestingly, they were also more likely to score high on a scale measuring altruism towards strangers.[18]

Any personality trait that's associated with psychopathy has its downsides, of course, and at the very least it might mean that some heroes may be brave and kind, but they are also sometimes show-offs who love to be the centre of attention. Still, it makes you think. Earlier in this book I challenged the notion that a kind action is diminished if the person who performs it feels good about themselves or even gains kudos from it. I certainly do not think it applies to acts of heroism which, after all, is why medals for gallantry exist and ceremonies honouring heroes take place. But beyond that, perhaps we should all try to learn from the 'fearlessly dominant' among us, to conquer our reluctance, awkwardness and embarrassment about intervening in difficult situations? And perhaps we need to conquer our fear of being misinterpreted that we saw in the Kindness Test?

In their work the psychologists Rachel Manning and Mark Levine have examined other reasons why people jump in to help. In one experiment, they recruited some Manchester United fans to take part and then arranged for a jogger in a park to pretend to trip and hurt their ankle. Sometimes the jogger was wearing a Liverpool football shirt, at other times a Manchester United one or a plain shirt. Happily, people passing by did sometimes stop and offer to help, but they were more likely to do so if the jogger was wearing a Manchester United shirt. Such is the strength of the shared identity engendered by football clubs.[19]

But what if like me, you don't care for the tribalism of football or, more seriously, you think it's important to help others irrespective of any difference, such as nationality or ethnicity? Is there not such a thing as shared *humanity*?

Commuters aren't generally regarded as having a strong group identity. They may be united in their dissatisfaction with the train service, but even so the behaviour they most often demonstrate is a strong desire to maintain their own private space, shutting out others and, yes, 'keeping themselves to themselves'. Yet in certain circumstances, individuals with no prior connection can be transformed into a collective, to the benefit of everyone. This has been demonstrated by Professor John Drury from the University of Sussex who analysed what happened after the London tube bombings in July 2005. Did people trample each other as they rushed to save themselves? No, they showed great concern for others. Were they selfish? No, they were considerate.

The researchers collected witness accounts from newspapers, blogs, radio documentaries and official reports, and even advertised for witnesses to tell them about their experiences. In a total of 287 accounts, there were just 18 mentions of anyone behaving selfishly (in interviews the criticism was that a few individuals were glued to their phones, or seemed to be in a world of their own, not that they pushed past other passengers). There were 207 stories of people helping each other, with people staying to help despite the fear that there might be another explosion or that the tunnel might collapse. They created makeshift bandages, tied tourniquets, comforted injured passengers, offered them water, helped them to get up and showed them the way out. The instant the bomb went off, the people inside the trains were no longer a group of random people; as one put it they 'were all in the same boat', or the same carriage rather, linked together by finding themselves in the same terrible situation. It was not a group identity they possessed before the attack or one that any of them would have chosen, but it was a group identity they all had in the moment. They were now part of a psychological crowd and that fostered deep mutual cooperation.[20]

Of course, one serious worry that many of us have is that if we were to intervene, in a fight say, the aggressor might turn on us and we might get seriously hurt. We've all read of stories like that of Kevin Alderton.

Kevin was a sergeant in the British Army when in May 1998, he saw two men attacking a woman in a doorway in London. Kevin and a friend intervened, but were soon surrounded and attacked by a much larger group of men. During the assault one of these men tried to gouge Kevin's eyes out. Although the injury to Kevin's eyes was very serious, initially he thought his sight would be fine. Within days, however, he went almost totally blind.

Kevin has since rebuilt his life, becoming the world record holder for blind speed skiing and touring the world as a motivational speaker. Like so many heroes, he says he doesn't regret his actions, despite the exceptionally high price he paid for getting involved.[21]

Stories like these capture the headlines and lead the police to advise us not to intervene, but rather to call them. In most situations this is probably good advice, but there's some evidence that we overestimate the chances of getting hurt ourselves if we step in to stop acts of aggression we witness. An interesting study in 2020 carefully coded CCTV footage from incidents in Amsterdam, Cape Town and Lancaster. It found that when two people were fighting and a third bystander intervened – perhaps holding back one of the fighting people or putting their body between the two assailants – in 96.4% of cases the 'have-a-go' hero was unharmed.[22] The 3.6% who were hurt were either hit once or shoved several times, not generally injured seriously. The age of the person stepping in made no difference, but the aggressor was more likely to hit the bystander who intervened if they knew that person (maybe they were the ones who stepped forward in the most dangerous situations despite the risk). In the case of complete strangers intervening, the chances of being hurt turned out to be very small.

In citing this study, I'm certainly not trying to encourage people to be reckless about their own safety, just suggesting that our instinct to help people in trouble – which I believe is strong in all of us – can be acted on safely in certain circumstances.

But thinking back for a moment to those more everyday moments of heroism and kindness, I'm still struck by the main barrier that people gave in the Kindness Test: their fear of being misinterpreted. This finding led me to look back at the Kindness Diary I'd been keeping and I noticed a pattern;

occasions where I'd thought about doing something kind and then not followed it through.

I live near one of the busiest railway stations in the country that still doesn't have escalators or lifts, so I quite often help people carry buggies up to the platforms – always a little too precariously for my liking. I'm terrified that I'm not balancing the buggy quite right and that I'll send the toddler tumbling down the concrete steps. Though so far that hasn't happened, I'm always pleased when we make it to the platform in one piece. In this case, the task is clearly defined with a start and an end, and I know what's required of me. But in my diary there are many instances where I'm not sure what to do.

Wednesday 6.45 p.m.

In an underground car park unlocking my bike when I see a woman using a tiny bike pump to try to pump up her tyres. I can hear the air hissing, so it's not really going into the tyres. Should I help? Would I even be any better at it? Would she think I thought she couldn't do it by herself because she's a woman? I decided I'd like someone to offer me help in that situation, so I say, 'Are you having any luck?' and ask whether she's tried the big bike pump that lives in the car park. She tries that. It works better. Should I stay until she's done it? It's dark and I'm hungry, so really I want to get going. I've got a 45-minute cycle ahead of me. So I ask if it's working. She says it is and I wish her luck. Kind in one way because I showed her the better pump, but not that kind because I didn't offer to do it for her. On that very same spot a few years ago my chain came off my bike and another woman cheerfully tipped my bike upside down, and put it back on for me, then wiped her oil-covered hands clean on her smart black trousers. Now that was kind.

Looking through the diary, I see there's a pattern. I'm often confused about exactly what's going on and hesitate before offering help, in case I've got it wrong. Like the people who took part in the Kindness Test, I don't want to be misinterpreted and I don't want to look stupid. I think I fall into a category I've decided to call: the hesitant helper. Take this entry from November 2021.

Wednesday 9.15 a.m.
Cycling to work. Am thinking how cold it is when I notice a man of about 30 on the other side of the road, walking fast in the opposite direction from me. He's wearing shorts and flip-flops. Brave choice in this weather, I think. He calls out, 'Lola!' to someone ahead of him. I cycle on and the cars ahead of me brake suddenly as a little terrier runs across the road. A woman in a raincoat beckons to it, calling, 'Poochy, poochy!'

Risky to let a dog off the lead on this busy road, I thought, and cycled on. Now you may have put this jigsaw of events together quicker than I did. But a while later, by which time I was far away, I connected the dots. The man is wearing shorts and flip-flops because he isn't intending to go out into the cold. His dog has escaped and must be Lola. He's gone searching in the wrong direction, and the reason raincoat woman is calling the dog 'Poochy' and not a better name, is that she doesn't know the dog, but is trying to save it from running back across the road. I've worked it out! I could be a detective! Just a rather slow one. Can I turn back and find the dog and put it in my basket, find the man and save the day? Will he think I'm trying to steal the dog? Will the woman think I'm trying to steal the dog? By now I have to accept that I'm far too far away to be any use. I've taken too long to work out what was going on and too hesitant to help.

It's like the mattress story all over again. I'm too slow to help. Perhaps I need to act more decisively and decide in advance that I am going to offer to help in such circumstances, even if I risk a slight embarrassment if I've 'read the room' wrong. In most cases, I'll be helping strangers after all, so I won't see them again. Does it really matter that much if they think I'm a bit daft or I'm sticking my nose in where it's not wanted?

Planned heroism

Some years ago, I interviewed a psychology professor in New York called Harold Takooshian. Back in 1983, Takooshian published a paper which showed that one strategy we can use to help us intervene safely and successfully is to consider in advance what level of action we would be prepared to take in a given situation.[23]

If you witness a crime, for example, do you think you are physically capable of tackling the criminal? Perhaps running down the street, rugby tackling someone and sitting on them until the cops come is a bit beyond you because of your size and strength – I'm thinking of myself here – but how about making clear you are filming the incident on your phone in the hope this deters the criminal? Or what about shouting that you've seen what they're up to, but leaving them the chance to run away?

Takooshian says one of the main reasons that street crime persists is that criminals expect people not to get involved. It's unlikely petty thieves, pickpockets and graffiti artists have read the literature on the bystander effect, but they've seen it quite often in action – or rather in inaction. And they rely on it to get away with their wrongdoing.

This is particularly true in big cities, where citizens are hyper-alert about their own safety, but don't see – or don't *want* to see – danger when others are involved. In one study, Takooshian and his students pretended to break into cars on 330 occasions in New York City. The break-ins were all a 'one-person' job and the 'thief' made it obvious: scanning a row of parked cars, taking a coat hanger, spending a minute anxiously and clumsily using it to unlock the door and then removing either a TV, a camera, a radio or, in a sign of the times perhaps (this was the 1970s), a fur coat. It was all a set-up of course and the cars selected for the break-ins were owned by members of the research team. So, how many times would you guess anyone stopped the 'thief' or even said anything?

Twenty-one times! Yes, 21 out of 330. Even more astonishingly, when the thief was a woman, some people even offered them help, which was kind of kind, I guess.[24] Takooshian told me that one of the students was so annoyed that no one challenged her when she was clearly breaking into a car that she went up and said to people, 'Can't you see me?!'

Reading this you can probably remember an incident when you saw something that seemed wrong, you could have acted safely enough, but probably out of inertia or embarrassment as much as fear, you did nothing. The way to avoid that happening in the future, Takooshian would argue, is to remember the incident and calculate what you would be comfortable doing the next time something similar happens. In a much smaller way, it is to do what Matthew Croucher did in Afghanistan. If you remember, his bravery stemmed from him having been trained and prepared for a certain situation, and then having the presence of mind to put that training and preparation into action when the situation arose.

In all of this, I think it is possible – and without throwing up! – to assert that there is indeed a 'hero inside ourself', and if that doesn't feel true for you today, that may be because a situation hasn't presented itself or there has been some inhibiting factor that has held you back in the past, but which you could overcome in the future. An important element here is to constantly remind yourself that just as there is more kindness in the world than we sometimes think, so there is more heroism too – particularly of the 'everyday' sort.

LAST KIND ACT CARRIED OUT
FOR SOMEONE ELSE

The Kindness Test

I helped a friend with multiple sclerosis apply for a disability benefit.

I made the postman happier.

*The Big Issue seller was looking bright and happy, and I told her so.
She was delighted that I saw her as an individual, and cared about her.*

*Every week I make bread for three close friends, no bread machine,
they don't pay me.*

Delivered some groceries to someone isolating due to Covid.

*Photographed a baptism and created a photo album for a stranger
whose baby was being christened on Sunday.*

*I spent time with my grandson and played a throwing game whilst
chatting about return to school as he is anxious.*

I rubbed some oil on someone's insect bites.

*I smiled and said good morning to everyone I encountered coming
into the building at work.*

I took old newspapers to a neighbour for their cat's litter tray.

I let someone off the hook.

7

REMEMBER TO BE KIND
TO YOURSELF

Have a look at these statements. Do any of them sound like you?

- I fear that if I become kinder to and less critical of myself my standards will drop.
- I feel that I don't deserve to be kind and forgiving to myself.
- Getting on in life is about being tough rather than compassionate.
- When I try to feel kind and warm to myself I just feel kind of empty.

These statements are four of the fifteen which make up a scale devised by a leading authority on shame and compassion, Professor Paul Gilbert, who I mentioned in Chapter 5 when I was looking at compassion for others. Gilbert came up with the statements as a result of the conversations he had with clients over many years. The scale has been tested on thousands of people and provides a reliable way of measuring our fears of extending kindness and compassion towards ourselves.[1] So, how did you do?

If you agree strongly with all four statements, it's likely you're wary of being kind to yourself, though you'd have to complete the whole scale to be sure. You may well be kind and compassionate towards others, but you struggle to apply the same compassion to yourself. When things go wrong in your life, an inner voice says far harsher words to yourself than you'd ever dream of saying to a friend in the same situation. You don't just avoid self-compassion; you fear it. You feel it is a weakness, an impediment.

One manifestation of this tendency can, as so often, be seen in the brain. In one study, volunteers were put in a brain scanner and asked to imagine themselves in a series of situations in which things had gone wrong, such as receiving a third job rejection in a row in the post. They were then asked how much they blamed themselves for the negative outcome. Neuroscientists found that the volunteers who were highly self-critical showed increased activity in two particular areas of the brain – the lateral prefrontal cortex and the dorsal anterior cingulate – areas associated with, among other things, detecting and resolving errors.[2] Meanwhile volunteers who were more inclined not to blame themselves had a different pattern of brain activity. In their case, the parts of the brain that were engaged were the insula and the left temporal pole, which are associated, again among other things, with feeling compassion towards others and with complex emotions such as pride or embarrassment respectively.

What, though, can we read into these differences in brain activity? The main thing, it turns out, is not the nature of differences, but the fact that there *are* clear differences between people who criticised themselves versus those who offered themselves comfort. It doesn't seem surprising that there are also appreciable and significant divergences in other ways, some of which can have a profound impact on our lives, as we shall see.

The selfless person, who always puts others first and themselves last, is often seen as the exemplar of kindness. But in this chapter, I will show that you can be kind to others *and* to yourself. Self-care doesn't need to slip into self-indulgence and self-obsession but rather, practised in a balanced way, it can put you in a place where your sense of well-being helps you to help others.

The perils of being hard on yourself

Some self-criticism is fine, of course. We all make mistakes, get things wrong and behave badly from time to time. If we simply ignored these occasions and forgave ourselves immediately, we wouldn't learn and grow and change as human beings. But if we are overly self-critical, the consequences can be serious. When all the best studies on self-compassion were brought together in an Australian meta-analysis, it was found that people who fear it experience more shame, anxiety, depression and distress than people who are kind to themselves.[3] Paul Gilbert's research has produced similar findings, also showing that those lacking in self-compassion tend to have difficult relationships with others.[4]

For anyone already experiencing depression, a lack of self-kindness can compound their suffering. Depressed people tend to be harder on themselves, believing that they are unlovable, useless at everything – and always will be. In this way, self-criticism can contribute to the downward spiral into despair. But a lack of compassion towards yourself can also be a starting point for depression, with research showing that self-criticism is a factor that is strikingly predictive of the condition. Indeed, one study showed that being big on self-criticism can predict more than a third of cases of depression, making it a more important factor than any other.[5] By contrast, the best studies on self-compassion and well-being show clearly that people with higher levels of self-compassion tend to have fewer mental health difficulties.[6]

The Kindness Test concurs with these studies. It found that people who are kind to themselves have higher well-being scores and higher life satisfaction, while those who are self-critical are more likely to feel lonely and to have mental health difficulties. Even more strikingly, the test showed that the people who were kindest to themselves observed more kindness around them in everyday life and even said that they received more acts of kindness from other people.

Other studies have added to the impressive list of benefits of self-compassion. People who are kind to themselves are less likely to ruminate (worry away in their minds about negative things), are less likely to be overly perfectionist and fear failure less. At the same time, on average they are more likely than other people to have higher levels of wisdom, curiosity, initiative, happiness and optimism.[7]

Given all this, it is worrying that a lack of compassion for ourselves appears to be quite widespread, particularly among certain groups. When adults in five Dutch cities completed questionnaires about their levels of compassion, on average women showed higher levels of compassion for other people than men did, but that didn't spread to themselves. In fact they had significantly higher levels of coldness towards themselves than men did. Meanwhile the fewer years people had spent in education, the more compassion they showed to others, but the less they showed to themselves.[8] We have to ask ourselves what's happening here. Are people made to feel that because they left school early and didn't go to university they don't deserve to be kind to themselves? Are we bringing up girls to believe that it's important to be kind to others, but that it would be somehow wrong to show themselves the same kindness?

Levels of self-compassion really matter. They have even been found to make a difference to how people managed during the pandemic. In one study, interviews were conducted with 4,000 people in 21 different countries during April and May 2020, while many of the participants were living through lockdowns. Across every country featured, people who feared self-compassion scored higher on measures of depression, anxiety and stress.[9] Another study, by the same authors, showed that people who were kind to themselves were not only less upset, but also less afraid of Covid-19.[10]

When something as huge as a global pandemic takes place, over which an individual has no control, it might be hard to believe that something as small as being kind to yourself can make a difference – and yet the data shows that it can and does. I wonder whether part of the explanation is that some people found it hard to acknowledge that they were suffering. How often did you have a lockdown conversation on Zoom or another platform in which someone you hadn't seen for some time asked you how you were managing? If you were like me, perhaps you paused, sighed and said something like: 'Well, you know . . .' only to follow this up with a quick: 'But of course I've got nothing to complain about compared with other people.' Suddenly, just having a job, a garden, not being ill, having family and friends who were still alive, gave you no right to be unhappy at all; indeed, you were obliged to feel lucky and even blessed.

The problem with feeling this way, even if it is impressively stoical, is that it can be a denial of the truth. Many people who were objectively fortunate during the pandemic – and I was certainly one – still felt cut off from people, constrained by the restrictions, and deeply anxious. We also felt self-pitying for feeling this way, which made our unhappiness worse still. What we needed to do, but of course wasn't easy, was to cut ourselves some slack when it came to self-compassion. OK, we hadn't had a close relative die of Covid, we hadn't been hospitalised by the virus, we hadn't lost our business because of lockdown, but in our own way we were suffering. We had all experienced a loss; the loss of life as we knew it. There was no shame in admitting that and looking for ways to support ourselves through a difficult time.

But people can prove resistant to such entreaties. Paul Gilbert has found that those who are afraid of self-compassion tend to actively resist any attempt by others to encourage them to be more kind to themselves. A classic example is doctors who may show huge compassion towards others, who know the value of kindness for good health and well-being, but who can be very hard on themselves – and who are not good at taking their own medicine if that involves prescribing themselves a bit more self-TLC. How then can self-compassion sceptics be convinced to be kinder to themselves? (Doctors, please note.)

More than just me

As I've shown, there is clear evidence that people who are kind to themselves have better psychological health. And if that's not enough, there are also reputable studies showing that self-compassion helps people stick to diets, smoke fewer cigarettes, exercise more, cope with chronic pain or survive a divorce. The evidence for the benefits of self-compassion is, in fact, overwhelming.

And yet, you may still have a niggling feeling – particularly if you are of a certain generation – that all this self-love and me-first is a bit soft and slippery. Surely if you are thinking of yourself, forgiving yourself and being kind to yourself, you risk becoming wet, self-indulgent and selfish?

Of course, at its worst the notion of self-care does invite criticism and even ridicule. And to be clear, I'm not suggesting that we should all be devoting hours of our day to excessive 'me-time' in which we luxuriate in hot baths, full of restorative oils, surrounded by expensive scented candles. We need more kindness in the world, but it is not going to come about if all we do is pamper ourselves in spa resorts or listen to self-help podcasts that urge us to focus on ourselves above all else. I'm with you if you feel irritated if a celebrity announces that their resolution for the year ahead is to 'love myself a lot more'. But on the other hand, there's nothing wrong with a *bit* of self-pampering, and certainly not in having a few hot baths (I'm a great fan myself!). And not the least of the reasons I'm an advocate for self-care is that the evidence suggests that a healthy amount of it can make a difference to the way we treat others. Simply put, people are better able to be kind to others if they start by being kind to themselves.

The teachings of Tibetan Buddhism are useful in this regard. Self-compassion within Buddhist thought is not simply a case of viewing yourself kindly. You may be experiencing struggle and pain, but you need to try to appreciate that this is a feeling common to all human beings. By acknowledging your own suffering, you are therefore acknowledging the shared suffering of humanity. From this perspective, showing warmth, tenderness and understanding towards yourself is an essential first step towards showing the same compassion to others.[11]

For a start, self-compassion can put you in a position where you have the energy to treat other people kindly. It's rather like that instruction you get on planes that you should put your own oxygen mask on first, before helping others. You're better able to assist someone else if you're not worrying about yourself. Of course, that is not to say that people who tend to neglect their own well-being are incapable of kindness. In fact, in the Kindness Test we found that people with depression can be notably kind, with participants who said they had mental health difficulties indicating they were more likely than non-depressed people to donate their time to help others and more inclined to give a higher proportion of a windfall to a good cause. But the fact is these respondents have such difficult lives that they are required to work very hard to show altruism. It doesn't always follow of course, but people who are able to be kind to themselves, who are less oppressed by self-criticism, can find themselves in a psychological state where it's easier to think of others.

Being kind to yourself doesn't automatically make you

kind to others, of course. But it can. A study in Australia is among the research that has shown a link. Two thousand teenagers were followed through their last three years of school and at different times their self-compassion and empathy were measured.[12] To work out who was the kindest among them the research team asked each student to name privately the three girls and the three boys in their English class who were always ready to lend a helping hand. This enabled the team to rank the students in order of how kind other students considered them to be. And the results were clear. The higher the students scored on 'kindness to themselves', the higher their scores on empathy towards others and the more likely they were to make it onto the kind classmate list.

There are also studies that show, for example, that people with high levels of self-kindness demonstrate more compassion for humanity, have more harmonious relationships and are more likely to apologise if they behave badly.[13] I should say though that not every piece of research finds that being kind to yourself makes you kinder to others. Notably, in our Kindness Test there was only a small association between being kind to others and kind to yourself. But we did find that being kind to others was only associated with lower levels of burnout if people were also compassionate to themselves.

And let's not forget, there's a case for being kind to yourself in and of itself. And here I'm going to go a bit guru-like and compose my own self-compassion motto:

If you think it's important to be kind to people, remember you are a person too, so don't neglect being kind to yourself.

But what is that sound I hear? Is it some of you grinding your teeth in irritation? I know there are people who read stuff like this and think that it's just an excuse for being lazy, selfish and narcissistic. I understand this concern, but I do want to push back a bit. First, remember that self-compassion should not be confused with self-esteem or self-aggrandisement. I'm not suggesting that you go around boasting about your achievements or basking in your own brilliance. I'm not saying you should think you are better than other people, or that thinking of number one puts you at the top of the charts. In fact, it is the opposite. It's about accepting that you are just like other people. Like them, you sometimes struggle and you sometimes feel pain. Accepting that fact is not self-indulgent, it is showing due tenderness towards yourself, as you would to anyone else in a similar situation.

Research conducted in the US, for example, which used scales measuring various aspects of personality, found there was an association between high scores on narcissism and self-esteem, but people who were high on self-compassion were no more likely than anyone else to be narcissistic.[14] A caring friend doesn't condemn you when you fall short; they try to encourage you. You can do the same for yourself.

Don't be your own harshest critic

What's the worst thing that has happened to you in the last four days that was your own fault? How about the worst thing that wasn't your fault? These are the questions that Mark Leary from Duke University in the US asked people by email several times over a three-week period.[15] He wanted to know whether self-compassion might help people to handle setbacks more effectively and his results suggested this was indeed true. The respondents who scored high on a self-compassion scale dealt with negative events with more equanimity than those who had low scores. They were also able to keep the setback in perspective even when it was their own fault, and at the same time were able to appreciate that their situation wasn't unique or any worse than things other people experience. All in all, the study demonstrated that people who are kind to themselves are better able to handle adversity by putting it into its proper perspective.

Mark Leary's next experiment was a bit meaner. This time people had to sit in front of a video camera and give a three-minute talk without any prep time, on a topic such as their hometown, or their plans for the future, or what they do and don't like about college. Each volunteer was told that another participant in the next room would be watching the talk and giving feedback. In fact, the feedback was fake and bore no relation to how well the person performed in any objective sense.

Entirely arbitrarily, exactly half the people were given positive scores, telling them the person assessing their talk scored them highly on skill, friendliness, likeability, intelligence and maturity. What more could you want? The other half were given neutral scores. That may not sound especially mean, but we have a tendency – demonstrated in numerous studies – to interpret neutral feedback as negative. Average scores tend to feel low. We want to be better than OK. So, trust me, it was quite mean.

After receiving the positive or not so positive feedback, the participants were then asked how they were feeling and how accurate they thought the rater had been. Those who were high in self-compassion coped better with receiving the neutral scores than those who were more self-critical, as you might expect by now, but what was really interesting was that they also handled the positive scores more evenly too, not letting this feedback sway how much they said they liked the observer. They'd had an ego boost, but they didn't let it go to their heads.

This is important, because it's not only the way you deal with negative feedback that matters in life. I'm reminded of something an actor friend of mine said that she was taught at drama school to prepare her for a career on the stage and on TV. If you get a bad review or any criticism, her tutor told her, then halve it in your mind. That way, it doesn't bring you down too much. But likewise, if you get a good review and are praised to the skies, you must halve that too. Life is full of ups and downs – for actors and the rest of us – and if you ride this rollercoaster too hard it will make you sick. We need instead to smooth out the bumps as much as we can and experience the highs and lows with a similar degree of level-headedness. Self-compassion, it seems, helps with that, so here's another reason to be kind to yourself.

Which is all well and good, but isn't there still a danger that even if you don't become narcissistic or overfull of yourself, this is a recipe for complacency, for a lazy, lackadaisical approach to life? Isn't there a value in being self-critical and demanding more of yourself? Of course, you still need to take setbacks seriously and to reflect on the part you might have played in them. But when we fail in an exam or go for a job interview and don't get the job, we have a tendency to focus too much on all the bad moments, dwelling on what we should have written or said, but didn't, or obsessing about possible screw-ups. To counterbalance this tendency, it's important to appreciate that there were almost certainly things we got right, where we gave smart answers and impressed the examiners or interviewers. OK, overall, we didn't do well, but we weren't a complete washout. We need to forgive ourselves for failing on this occasion, dust ourselves down and move on.

Evidence shows that this approach could help you to succeed next time. Here's a study to bring anyone who tends to put things off some cheer. Students at a university in Canada were asked whether they had put off studying for their exams until the last minute. Had they done less important things when they could have been revising? They were also followed over time. Not surprisingly the procrastinating students didn't tend to do that well (that's not the cheerful bit), but if they forgave themselves, when it came to the next exam, they were more likely to study hard than those who beat themselves up about it.[16]

Being kinder to yourself isn't necessarily easy

One route to greater self-compassion is to make more time for yourself so that you can do the things you like and which you find relaxing. In my last book *The Art of Rest* I explained how to draw up your own personal prescription for rest. In essence, you need to find the two or three activities that you personally find most restful, and then you need to find ways of incorporating them into your everyday life. This sounds easy enough, but is actually quite difficult because of the demands put on us, by ourselves and others, in modern society. Still, I've been gratified by the number of people who've read *The Art of Rest* and who've told me that making their own prescription for rest has really helped them. I've no doubt that more rest is one way of showing yourself true self-compassion, but there are others of course.

The titles of most papers in psychology journals can be quite dull, but I liked this one when I spotted it. It's called 'Do Unto Others or Treat Yourself?'[17] and it's a study by a Californian psychologist called Katherine Nelson. She recruited people online, randomly assigned them to one of four groups and instructed them to perform three kind acts the following day. One group directed their acts towards other individuals, the second was told to direct them towards humanity or the world, and the third group was asked to find three ways of being kind to themselves. The fourth group, the control group, simply kept a log of their activities on the day in question. Once a week for four weeks the instructions were repeated.

Before all this began the participants had filled in questionnaires to assess their well-being, including a measure I particularly like which looks at whether you are flourishing or languishing psychologically, going beyond the presence or absence of specific mental health problems to ask how their life was really panning out.

Now, for the purposes of this chapter Nelson's main finding may not sound helpful, because she found that doing nice things for yourself didn't make as much difference to well-being as doing them for other people. But of course, looking at the bigger picture, the subject this whole book is exploring, this conclusion is both positive and no great surprise. The kindnesses that participants were suggested to show themselves involved taking a five-minute break or treating themselves to a massage. These tended towards the hedonic. While the examples of kindness to others or the wider world were of more substance, such as cooking a meal for a friend or volunteering for a local organisation. These were acts that improve connections with others and are more eudaimonic – they have more meaning. In that spirit, a lesson from this study is that while cossetting yourself is lovely, it's not the same as showing true kindness to yourself. To make a lasting difference to our mental health, we need more than self-care. We need self-kindness of a deeper kind, which involves taking control of those critical voices in our heads and being more forgiving of ourselves.

How then to achieve something deeper? It is time for me to put on a strange outfit.

I start by dragging on thick, black, skin-tight leggings. Then I squeeze myself into a long-sleeved top which is just as close fitting. It feels a bit like a wetsuit and is not the most attractive of looks to be honest. Next a technician sticks little white blobs on my joints – elbows, wrists, ankles, knees (think Abba in the pictures of them in 2022 creating the avatars for their virtual concert).

Wearing this get-up, I enter a room. There are no windows and all the walls are blue. I'm surrounded by cameras, suspended from every corner of the ceiling, with some extras dotted around for luck. Now a large, heavy helmet is lowered onto my head, and with this fitted, I'm transported into an alternative reality. Not the jungles of the Amazon or the pyramids of Ancient Egypt or the mean streets of a videogame. Instead, what I see in the mirror in front of me is a life-sized avatar. This figure staring back at me doesn't look like me. For a start, she is wearing jeans and a belted cardigan. 'Wave your arms about. Do anything. We're training the avatar to match your movements,' a technician instructs me through the headphones in my helmet. I do as he says and soon whatever I do, the avatar does too. If I lift an arm, so does she. If I bend my knees, so does she. If I dance badly, so does she. Her body is so responsive to my movements that it begins to feel as though her body and mine are one. Even the shadows behind her move when I do.

This elaborate virtual reality set-up is tricking my brain into thinking the body opposite me in the mirror is mine. I know intellectually that it's not my body. We're not alike, and yet there's a powerful sense that it is me. I have embodied this other 'woman'.

Then suddenly someone else appears beside this other 'me'. Another avatar, but a smaller one. A child this time – a little girl with a brown ponytail and a fluorescent pink t-shirt. She's about eight or nine maybe? And she looks really upset. She has her hands over her face and is hunched over. I realise she is crying. I want to comfort her. But I was told before the experiment began that if I come across someone in need of comfort, I shouldn't use my own words, but instead I must read from a script. I try to say the words as kindly as I can. In a while the little girl stops crying. I think she's going to be OK.

And then in this shifting virtual world everything changes again. The avatar facing me is suddenly really large compared with me. As if she's a giant or I'm a child. Yes, that's it: for the first time in decades, I feel physically like a child. I'd forgotten what it was like to have adults towering over me

– and yet it quickly feels familiar. And then the tall woman looks down at me gently and starts saying my words back using my actual voice. 'It can be really hard when something happens like this that's upset you. Sometimes I find when I'm really upset, it can help if you think of someone who really loves you.'

It's as though I'm comforting myself. And it's very powerful and moving. It makes me feel warm and safe. Like a loved child.[18]

Now this may all sound very strange and perhaps a lot of fun, but it has a serious purpose. The whole set-up is part of a new kind of therapy for people prone to excessive self-criticism who are experiencing depression. It's been developed by researchers at University College London. But how can a clearly fake avatar speaking to you make a difference to something as real and debilitating as depression? The answer is that the experience is so immersive that it makes people feel as if they really are receiving compassion from themselves. As we've seen, many people with depression are hard on themselves, but this interaction with an avatar who moves and speaks like them, and shows them kindness and empathy, gives them a visceral experience of self-compassion, even if just for a few minutes.

My trial of the technology only lasted a short time, but an actual session would normally take about 45 minutes and in an initial, small trial, participants took part in three such sessions. The results were impressive. After completing these sessions, a month later, two thirds of the patients had lower levels of depression.[19] I can see why it can work. It was genuinely moving to experience compassion from a computerised version of myself. The memory of that warm feeling has stayed with me and helped in moments of doubt and darkness.

Other routes to self-kindness

Using avatars and virtual reality is cutting-edge stuff and needs more development before it becomes widely available, but there are other forms of therapy that are more accessible now which aim to help us to be kinder to ourselves. These include compassion-focused therapy, where therapists very carefully probe why people fear being kind to themselves. Role play can be helpful too. Participants sit in one chair and speak as their angry self. They then move to the empty chair opposite where their compassionate self is sitting. In this way they have a conversation between their two selves, the two sides of their personality. It sounds a bit weird, but it does achieve positive results.

Compassion-focused therapist Charlie Heriot-Maitland suggests a slightly different version of this technique. Imagine you are walking down a street as your compassionate self and you meet your sad self coming the other way. What would the compassionate self say to the sad self if the sad self was feeling low? Would they put their arm around them? Would they say something reassuring? Probably. So why not be kind to yourself in the same way?

I like a line from one of Nikita Gill's poems, 'Look at yourself the way someone who truly loves you does'. And Chris Johnstone, who runs resilience workshops, describes self-compassion as 'making an agreement to be an ally to yourself'. To take an example, when you're feeling guilty about having behaved badly, instead of beating yourself up about it, ask yourself why you acted in the way that you did. Maybe you replied to an email in a way that in retrospect was overly angry. How were you feeling at that moment and why might you have done it? Ask how your compassionate self might help? This doesn't mean letting yourself off. In fact, you can still put right what you did by, for example, apologising for that intemperate message.

You could even write a compassionate letter to the part of you that is struggling. Mark Leary tried this as part of his series of studies on how self-compassion can help people to deal with unpleasant events. First, participants had to think of a negative event from their past that made them feel bad about themselves and then, bearing that in mind, list the ways in which other people may have experienced similar events. This was to prompt feelings of shared humanity. Then participants were asked to write a paragraph expressing understanding, kindness and concern to themselves in the way they might write to a friend who'd experienced what they'd been through. Through this work, Leary demonstrated that it was possible to induce self-compassion, with participants who completed the exercises experiencing fewer negative emotions about the unpleasant event.[20] Interestingly, they were still more likely to think that they were the type of person to whom such negative events happened, and they still felt they'd made a real mistake – but the important difference was that they didn't hate themselves for it.

Charlie Heriot-Maitland suggests another way to increase your levels of self-compassion. Set yourself a self-kindness training plan, rather like you might do if you were trying to improve your physical fitness. So, one day you might write a compassionate letter to yourself, while on another you might set a few minutes aside for some quiet breathing exercises. The idea is to make commitments to be kind to yourself and to stick to them. You can still go to the gym or out jogging as well of course.

There are also carefully designed courses that can teach you how to be kinder to yourself. One method called mindful self-compassion was developed by a compassion researcher, Kristen Neff, and a clinical psychologist, Christopher Germer, both based in the US. It consists of weekly workshops for eight weeks where people practise – quite hard – being self-compassionate.

Participants learn mindfulness skills, are taught to remember that they're not the only person who suffers setbacks and are given techniques for treating themselves with more caring concern. Again, this is not about encouraging self-obsession. In fact, it's the opposite. Participants are urged not to focus on themselves too much, but to place their troubles in a wider perspective. The course has been trialled and the results were impressive. Straight afterwards, people's levels of mindfulness, self-compassion, life satisfaction and happiness had risen significantly and their feelings of depression, anxiety and stress had dropped, compared with a group of people who hadn't yet attended the course. The positive effects also had a lasting impact on well-being. You might suppose that after a few weeks people would go back to their old habits and start blaming themselves again. But no, a year after the course, the gains remained.[21]

The people who pioneered the workshops suggest similar techniques which you can try at home. Here's Christopher Germer's very practical suggestion for something you can do when you are upset after an argument, or when you're anxious or stressed or simply fed up. It's a simple three-step programme.

- Slow down, take a few deep breaths.
- Now place your hand on your heart.
- Then slowly say these sentences to yourself in a warm tone of voice: 'This is a moment of suffering. Suffering is part of everyone's life. May I be compassionate to myself in this moment.'[22]

It takes no time. You can do it in your head if you want to, without anyone even noticing. I've tried it many times and by showing myself a bit of compassion I immediately feel calmer and less stressed.

Of course, even if you do try out all these ideas and learn to be kinder to yourself, it won't mean you'll never feel angry or despondent or fearful or down in the dumps. Self-compassion is not about ridding yourself of negative emotions, even if this were possible. Sometimes it is appropriate and indeed important to feel angry or despondent or fearful or down in the dumps (see my first book *Emotional Rollercoaster*, for why we really do need all our emotions). And sometimes you'll feel this way because you really messed up. In which case, it is right to blame yourself. All I'm saying is that you should and can be proportionately self-critical. And if you are, you're likely to be kinder in the round.

LAST ACT OF KINDNESS RECEIVED

The Kindness Test

Someone stood in a queue to save my place so I didn't get wet and cold.

Birthday cards, emails, phone calls and visits from more than a hundred people. I had no idea that many people knew (or cared) that it was my birthday.

Walking in heavy shower when a stranger saved my brolly from blowing away.

A man was making huge bubbles on my city street corner.

My partner polished up a brass frame for my room and it looks amazing. I didn't ask him to do it.

A squeeze of my arm after a funeral when I was visibly upset.

Someone at work asked how I was and listened.

Cup of tea in bed!

My partner oiled my bike and pumped up the tyres.

At a meeting, passions are high and I find it impossible to interrupt. The facilitator makes a space and invites me to contribute.

My grown-up children walked at my pace.

A PRESCRIPTION FOR KINDNESS

I hope that this book has made you value kindness and appreciate its importance. If we could all be kinder to ourselves, to others and to wider society, the world would be a better place. It wouldn't solve everything of course, but might make things a little easier for a lot of people. Part of the reason why the world isn't kinder already is because it can be hard to be kind. I'm not saying it's easy or that I'm especially kind. Like everyone, I struggle with it.

With that in mind, in this conclusion I want to set out my 20 steps to a kinder world. It draws on all the scientific studies that have featured in the preceding chapters, synthesising the knowledge I've set out over more than 200 pages. Do feel free to pick and choose from the 20 tips. Not all of them will be relevant to you. But hopefully some of them will help you to become a kinder person, which in turn will make you a happier and more fulfilled person.

1. Become a kindness twitcher

If we think someone has been kind to us, we are more likely to be kind to them and to pay that kindness forward to others. So, a good place to start in making the world a kinder place is by recognising that it's already full of kindness. Inevitably unpleasant incidents and bad behaviour capture our attention and as a result it's easy to miss the fact that most of the time people are nice to each other. Try to counteract this negative tendency. So, for instance, if one of your work colleagues is nasty to you, try not to let that dominate your thoughts – make an effort to recall all the small acts of friendliness and helpfulness directed towards you at work and which you probably hardly noticed at the time. You may well find that your 'bad' day was actually full of kindness.

Like a bird watcher noting down each occasion on which they see a certain species, we could be on the lookout for instances of kindness, both the actions of others and ourselves. It has been shown that noting down positive moments every day is good for our mental well-being – and it would alert us to the fact that kindness is all around if only we look for it and appreciate it. So how about making a habit of recording at least one instance of kindness that you notice someone carrying out each day? It might be for you; it might be for someone else. But once you start looking out for kindness, you see it everywhere.

And don't forget to count your own acts of kindness in a list. When a study in Japan measured people's happiness levels and then asked them to count up the number of kind acts they carried out in a week, their happiness levels were found to have risen significantly compared with a control group.[1] So observe yourself being kind and you stand to benefit.

2. Don't assume children are thoughtless and selfish

From the terrible twos to teenage tantrums, it can be tempting to caricature children as selfish and inconsiderate. In fact, research shows that even toddlers – whose brains are early in development, making it hard for them to understand the perspective of others – are kinder than we think, sharing toys with other children and helping adults in difficulty, while a lot of the negative stereotypes around teenagers are unfair. It's true that on average people tend to get even kinder as they get older, but children and young people are often kind too and we should notice and nurture this behaviour. There's nothing wrong with praising kindness, rewarding it and above all encouraging it. And that goes for adults too.

3. Don't let the news get you down

The litany of conflict, violence, corruption and dishonesty in the daily news paints a false picture of reality. Sure, bad things happen in the world, but in fact humanity predominates over inhumanity. All the evidence shows that our era is on the whole characterised not by war, cruelty and selfishness, but rather by cooperation, civility and respect for others. Some people have suggested that we are left with such a warped view of the world via the media, that we should stop reading it, listening to it or watching it. That might be a step too far. The truth is it's crucial to understand the bad things that are happening, if we are to stand any chance of stopping them. On the other hand, doom-scrolling all day is not a good idea.

We should always put the news into perspective. Most of the time, the reason something is on the news is because it's rare, not because it's common. When you're living through an overwhelming negative news event, like a pandemic for example, keep yourself informed, but choose your sources carefully and limit your consumption to once or twice a day. If anything really urgent happens, someone is sure to tell you about it.

4. Enjoy the warm glow that comes from being kind to others

Studies have shown that if we perform kind acts, we enjoy measurable health benefits, both mental and physical. Behaving in kind ways reduces burnout, stress and social anxiety, improves our well-being and might even help us to live longer. Kind actions stimulate the same reward centres in our brain that are activated when we see someone we love, or are given chocolate or money. In other words, we get a lot out of being kind, both in the short and the long term. Some people feel guilty for feeling good about being kind. Fight that feeling. Bask in the warm glow of being kind. You deserve it. Kindness is not a matter of saintly sacrifice, but rather being a decent, cooperative human being who gains as well as gives.

5. Be a eudaimonic pleasure seeker as well as a hedonic one

The most obvious way to enjoy ourselves is by having as many pleasurable moments as possible through immediate sensory experience – in other words, to be a hedonist. But a more rounded person, and ultimately a more fulfilled one, focuses on living a more meaningful life by achieving their wider potential in life and acting in a virtuous way. This is called eudaimonia.

Being altruistic – not all the time, but as often as we can – is a great way to achieve eudaimonic pleasure in life. That doesn't mean that by being kind we can transform our lives completely. But studies show that even remembering kind acts we have performed in the past can enhance our sense of self and increase levels of well-being.

6. Get that extra boost by active volunteering

There is a strong social element to volunteering which brings added benefits to people who practise it, as well as those receiving the service. Many studies have shown that volunteering increases self-worth and self-confidence and boosts happiness. It is not some miracle cure for serious mental health problems, but it does give people a sense of purpose and meaning. It is a classic win/win activity.

So, if you don't volunteer already – and if you can fit it in with everything else you have to do – you could consider doing some voluntary activity in your community or beyond. Organisations are always on the lookout for volunteer trustees or governors to help oversee the work of charities or community organisations. Or you can be more hands-on, helping in practical ways at your local food bank or homeless centre. Whatever you decide to do, volunteering can foster connections with others and remind us of our shared humanity.

7. Remember: you can be kind and win

The kindness I'm interested in can be quite muscular. And you can still win. Being kind is not about being soft or gullible, but fair and consistent and trustworthy. It is about understanding other people and therefore being able to get the best out of them – and that's crucial for anyone leading a team or running an organisation. Many of the world's most successful people, in business and other fields, now see the value of kindness over ruthlessness.

This can involve moving away from a 'winning at all costs' mentality to seeing the bigger picture and recalibrating what constitutes success. Short-term profit margins might be important, but so is a loyal and committed work force and a sustainable business model. Apply these lessons to your own life, while remembering acting kindly sometimes involves hard decisions – in other words, tough love – as well as just 'being nice'.

8. Try to leave every situation a bit better than when you arrived

You can do this by making sure people feel noticed and appreciated, however fleeting your contact. And here I'll cheat by adding a tip, not from me, but from the Dalai Lama: 'I try to treat whoever I meet as an old friend. This gives me a genuine feeling of happiness.'

9. Channel your inner Atticus

Like Atticus Finch in *To Kill a Mockingbird* it is a good idea to try to see the best in people. I'm not pretending this is always easy. But people who disagree with you or have different world-views are not idiots and villains (not most of the time, anyway) and if you took the trouble to see things from their point of view, you'd come to appreciate that. Try – in the jargon – to enhance your empathic responsivity and place yourself in the position of others. Don't be afraid to empathise. It's human.

10. Practise active empathy

To enhance the empathy that lies behind a lot of kindness takes active effort. It also takes time and requires humility. First you may need to overcome sheer inertia and invest energy in understanding why you should see things as others do. You might need to show compassion towards them, compassion that at first sight you might think they don't deserve. What in their life and circumstances might explain, if not excuse, their actions or their plight?

One way to become more empathic is to view it as a skill you can develop, like gardening or playing the piano. You could look into having some 'compassion training' or take time to learn a few kindness meditation techniques.

Studies have shown that through such training people not only feel more empathic towards those who are suffering, but more energised to do something to relieve that suffering.

11. Don't make kindness another job on your to-do list

Take kindness seriously, but not so seriously that you start to feel weighed down by the need to be kind. It can be incorporated into your life without huge disruption. You don't need to have lots of time. You don't have to change the world (although don't let me stop you if that was your plan). Even saying a few kind words that take no time can make a difference to the people you live and work with.

12. Read, read seriously

There is an easy way of seeing inside the minds of other people, one in which other people's thoughts and feelings are laid out for you like a book. In fact they *are* books. Reading, fiction in particular, allows us to see perspectives other than our own, which teaches us empathy and which in turn increases mutual kindness.

13. Listen, really listen

People like to be listened to – just that.

14. Start conversations with strangers

They like it, they really do. It will brighten their day and yours.

15. Take an awe walk

This simply means going for a walk and deliberately looking around for things that strike awe in you. The awe-inspiring thing could be a mighty building made by humans or a decomposing leaf with an intricate skeleton – anything that reminds you how wonderful the world can be. It wouldn't be fair to start making you read about a whole new study at this late juncture in the book, so you'll have to trust me on this one, but people in the study who took regular awe walks had more feelings of empathy and concern for others.[2] They also saw a drop in the mental distress they experienced.

16. Pause before you post

Social media can be a cesspit of cruelty and hatred, and even when it's not quite that bad, it's often just an echo chamber of your existing views or a place where deliberately provocative posts are given greater prominence. This can reinforce notions that people who disagree with you must be stupid and wicked.

To overcome this tendency – which distorts reality – stop and think before you respond angrily to a post that you strongly disagree with. Think to yourself how you would react if the post had come from a friend or family member. Most likely, you'd moderate your response in this case, so why not do so in all situations?

Better still, follow the old advice – 'if you can't say something nice, don't say anything at all'. Why message someone to tell them their project/book/TV programme is no good? They've probably tried really hard. They probably know its shortcomings – and is your comment really going to teach them anything useful?

17. Make kindness the key to who you follow and unfollow on social media

One of the reasons social media can be so full of cruelty, anger and spite is because the people who post such stuff seem to attract more followers, more likes and more comments. The algorithms promote the most popular. This leads them to rise to the top and gives them more visibility – and so the negative cycle ratchets up inexorably. But it's up to us who gets our vote. We get to choose who we promote on feeds, so we can start a fightback against anger, negativity and rudeness. If we all decided to ignore these keyboard warriors and instead seek out, follow, engage with and share posts from the people who say wise, positive and kind things then the good would start to outnumber the bad. So, start today by unfollowing anyone who uses social media to make the world a more unkind place.

18. Make plans to be a hero (because you never know when you might be one)

You probably don't think you'll ever be a real hero. As I've said, research suggests that on average a person will face fewer than six emergency situations in a lifetime. On the other hand, those people who do intervene to save others, sometimes putting their own lives in peril, almost always suggest that anyone in their place would have done the same. So there is a real chance that at some point in your life you'll be faced with a situation where you could intervene to help someone in the most profound act of kindness possible. How, though, do you ensure that your intervention makes things better, not worse?

Research suggests that the best strategy to increase the chances that you will act safely and successfully is to think in advance about the action you'd be prepared to take in a given situation. If you see someone struggling in deep water, and you know it's not safe for you to jump in to try to save them – maybe you could throw something to them or take the lead in contacting the emergency services?

By making plans for various scenarios, you will be following the example of professionals like soldiers and police officers who train to react to different emergencies, and then are able to act effectively if and when the situation arises.

19. Be kind to yourself

To be truly kind you need to put others first and yourself last, right? Wrong. If you neglect your own well-being, you'll face burnout, and then you'll have less energy and scope to show kindness to others. Self-care, practised in a balanced way, is not the slippery slope to selfishness, but rather the starting point for caring about others. Indeed, by acknowledging that you sometimes suffer and feel pain, you're not – or shouldn't be – thinking you're somehow special. Rather, you're acknowledging that you are sharing – however small or large your portion may be – in the suffering and pain of humanity.

20. Be true to yourself when you are kind

We can't all be Abie and donate our kidneys to strangers. He didn't mind undergoing surgery. You, on the other hand, might feel this is a step too far. And that's fine. It's better to be kind in the way that suits you best rather than do nothing. So if your way of showing kindness is to truly listen to people or to talk to strangers or to donate money, then don't beat yourself up for the choices you're not making. Maybe choose to use a particular skill you have; the thing that you find easy and others find hard. Every one of us can be kind in our own way.

ACKNOWLEDGEMENTS

For a while I've been wanting to write a book about kindness because I constantly marvel at the kind things people do for each other. Now feels like the right time for this book because the world feels in need of some kindness (or maybe it always feels like that, regardless of when you live).

It's also been the perfect timing because when I began this book I had just been invited by the University of Sussex to become a Visiting Professor, which meant returning to the university where I was an undergraduate, but that also has the newly created Sussex Centre for Research on Kindness.

I had already begun researching this book when Professor Robin Banerjee and I discussed the idea of carrying out a large-scale piece of research to examine what people think about kindness.

Thank you to Mohit Bakaya and Dan Clarke from BBC Radio 4 for their enthusiasm when I suggested a collaboration between the BBC and the University of Sussex.

It's been a real pleasure to work closely with Robin Banerjee and Gillian Sandstrom who succeeded in creating a big study in a short amount of time. It was thanks to their hard work and to this long list of people that it was possible to get it up and running so fast: Dan Cullen, Lucie Crowter, Jenny

Gu, Maruša Levstek, Kate Cavanagh, Clara Strauss, Rona Hart, Daniel Campbell-Meiklejohn, Michelle Lefevre, Anne-Meike Fechter, Zahira Jaser, Michael Banissy, Jo Cutler, Pat Lockwood and Masaki Yuki.

Robin has responded patiently every single time I've interrupted him with yet another query about the study and Danielle Evans did a great job with him in analysing the data.

We had no idea that so many people would complete the questionnaires and I'm grateful to the 60,000 people who gave up their time to do so; an act of kindness in itself.

The preliminary results were broadcast in a series I presented on Radio 4 called *The Anatomy of Kindness*, which was produced by Geraldine Fitzgerald and Erika Wright, two incredibly talented science producers who are always wonderful to work with. Thank you to everyone I interviewed about kindness for the series.

The Kindness Test is just one of the many, many research studies I draw on in this book. I get to see at close quarters how much hard work is involved in setting up any research and I'm grateful to all the psychologists and neuroscientists who take the time to do the research that the rest of us can learn from.

At Kindfest 2020 I met (virtually) many people who had wise words to say on kindness, some of whom I've included in this book. Thank you to its founder, Susie Hills, who does a great job bringing together thousands of people who believe in kindness.

It turns out that everyone studying kindness is very kind (which is apt). When I emailed to ask researchers if they could share their scientific papers, replies came within minutes. Thank you to the people whose work has, alongside that of the Sussex team, particularly influenced my thinking on kindness: Paul Gilbert, Sara Konrath, John-Tyler Binfet, Jamil Zaki, John Price, Daniel Batson, Michael Brown, Oliver Scott Curry and Lee Rowland. And there are dozens more that you'll find in the endnotes.

Thank you to everyone who has shared their personal stories with me.

I'm very grateful to Lorna Stewart who has been painstaking in checking the details of the experiments I've described. Anything that's not quite right now, is definitely my mistake. And thank you to Daniel Campbell-Meiklejohn for his help in my descriptions of the brain.

Canongate are wonderful publishers – both enthusiastic and efficient. Special thanks to Lucy Zhou, Alice Shortland, Jenny Fry, Leila Cruickshank and Vicki Rutherford, and especially to my editor Simon Thorogood whose suggestions are always wise. He definitely made this book so much better, along with the meticulous, patient copy editor Gabrielle Chant.

And thank you to my agent Will Francis at Janklow & Nesbit. Along with his colleagues Ren Balcombe and Kirsty Gordon, he provides everything an author could want from a great agent.

Finally thanks to my husband, Tim, who took the time to read my first drafts and always had good ideas for improving them. Very kind of him.

NOTES

This list is not exhaustive, but these are the main research papers to which I refer in *The Keys to Kindness*. Apologies to third and fourth and in one case forty-fourth authors, but to save space and trees, where there are multiple authors, I've only included the first here. I've abbreviated Journal to 'J' and psychology to 'psych'. I hope you can find what you are looking for. There are some truly fascinating studies here.

Online sources listed below were accessed in June 2022.

Introduction

1   For an excellent and comprehensive review of research on the benefits of kindness and empathy see Konrath, S. & Grynberg, D. (2016) 'The Positive (and Negative) Psychology of Empathy'. In Watt, D.F. & Panksepp, J. (Eds.), *Psychology and Neurobiology of Empathy*. New York: Nova Biomedical Books

2   Penner, L.A. et al (2008) 'Parents' Empathic Responses and Pain and Distress in Pediatric Patients'. *Basic and Applied Social Psych*, 30(2), 102–13

1 There is more kindness in the world than you might think

1   Côté, S.M. et al (2006) 'The Development of Physical Aggression from Toddlerhood to Pre-adolescence: A Nationwide Longitudinal Study of Canadian Children.' *J. of Abnormal Child Psych*, 34, 71–5

2   Hammond, C.A. (2016) *Mind Over Money: The Psychology of Money and How to Use it Better.* Edinburgh: Canongate

3   Ulber, J. et al (2015) 'How 18- and 24-month-old Peers Divide Resources Among Themselves'. *J. of Experimental Child Psych*, 140, 228–244

4   Hepach, R. et al (2017) 'The Fulfillment of Others' Needs Elevates Children's Body Posture'. *Developmental Psych*, 53(1), 100–13

5   Zahn-Waxler, C. et al (1992) 'Development of Concern for Others'. *Developmental Psych*, 28(1), 126–36

6   Warneken, F. & Tomasello, M. (2009) 'The Roots of Human Altruism'. *British Journal of Psych,* 100(3), 455–71

7   Ulber, J. & Tomasello, M. (2020) 'Young Children's Prosocial Responses Toward Peers and Adults in Two Social Contexts'. *J. of experimental child psych, 198*, 104888

8   Binfet, J.T. (2016) 'Kindness at School: What Children's Drawings Reveal About Themselves, Their Teachers, and Their Learning Communities'. *J. of Childhood Studies*, 41, 29–42

9   Binfet, J.T. & Enns, C. (2018) 'Quiet Kindness in School: Socially and Emotionally Sophisticated Kindness Flying Beneath the Radar of Parents and Educators'. *J. of Childhood Studies*, 43, 31–45

10   Choudhury, S. et al (2006) 'Social Cognitive Development During Adolescence'. *Social Cognitive and Affective Neuroscience*, 1(3), 165–74

11   Binfet, J.T. (2020) 'Kinder Than We Might Think: How Adolescents Are Kind'. *Canadian J. of School Psych*, 35(2), 87–99

12   Hammond (2016), *Mind Over Money*

13 Lockwood, P.L. et al (2021) 'Aging Increases Prosocial Motivation for Effort'. *Psychological Science*, 32(5), 668–81

14 Thomas, G. & Maio, G.R. (2008) 'Man, I Feel Like a Woman: When and How Gender-role Motivation Helps Mind-reading'. *J. of Personality and Social Psych*, 95(5), 1165–79

15 Klein, K.J.K. & Hodges, S.D. (2001) 'Gender Differences, Motivation, and Empathic Accuracy: When It Pays to Understand'. *Personality and Social Psych Bulletin*, 27, 720–30

16 The Light Triad test can be found here: https://scottbarrykaufman.com/lighttriadscale/.

17 Hazlitt, W. (1900) 'My First Acquaintance with Poets'. In Carr, F. (Ed.) *Essays of William Hazlitt*. London: Walter Scott

18 Stanley Milgram quoted in Perry, G. (2012) *Behind the Shock Machine*. Victoria, Australia: Scribe, 325

19 For the whole story you can listen to my documentary *Mind Changers* on BBC Radio 4, produced by Marya Burgess, 7 May 2008: https://www.bbc.co.uk/programmes/b00b529r.

20 The story of West Ham footballer Kurt Zouma being prosecuted after a video of him kicking his cat went viral was covered in numerous news outlets including the *Metro*, 24 May 2022: https://metro.co.uk/2022/05/24/west-ham-footballer-kurt-zouma-pleads-guilty-to-kicking-his-cat-16699293/.

21 Pinker, S. (2011) *The Better Angels of Our Nature*. London: Penguin, xx

22 Pinker, *Better Angels* 2011, 91

23 Zarins, S. & Konrath, S. (2017) 'Changes Over Time in Compassion-Related Variables in the United States'. In Seppälä, E.M. et al. *The Oxford Handbook of Compassion Science*

24 Bartlett, M.Y. & DeSteno, D. (2006) 'Gratitude and Prosocial Behavior: Helping When It Costs You'. *Psychological Science*, 17(4), 319–25

25 A brief biography of Benjamin Webb can be found on this website: https://www.geographicus.com/P/ctgy&Category_Code= webbbenjamin.

26 Letter from Benjamin Franklin to Benjamin Webb, dated 22 April 1784. Transcript, Library of Congress: https://founders.archives. gov/documents/Franklin/01-42-02-0117

27 Gray, K. et al (2014) 'Paying It Forward: Generalized Reciprocity and the Limits of Generosity'. *J. of Experimental Psych: General*, 143(1), 247–54

28 Goldstein, N.J. et al (2008) 'A Room With a Viewpoint: Using Social Norms To Motivate Environmental Conservation in Hotels'. *J. of Consumer Research*, 35(3), 472–82

29 Kraft-Todd, G.T. et al (2018) 'Credibility-enhancing Displays Promote the Provision of Non-normative Public Goods'. *Nature*, 563, 245–8

2 Being kind makes you feel good and that's OK

1 Chancellor, J. et al (2018) 'Everyday Prosociality in the Workplace: The Reinforcing Benefits of Giving, Getting, and Glimpsing'. *Emotion*, 18(4), 507–17

2 Dunn, E.W. et al (2008) 'Spending Money on Others Promotes Happiness'. *Science*. 319(5870), 1687–8

3 Aknin L.B. et al (2013) 'Prosocial Spending and Well-being: Cross-cultural Evidence for a Psychological Universal'. *J. of Personality & Social Psych* 104(4), 635–52

4 Choi, N.G. & Kim, J. (2011) 'The Effect of Time Volunteering and Charitable Donations in Later Life on Psychological Well-being'. *Ageing & Society*, 31(4), 590–610. Also for an excellent review of work done in this area see Konrath, S. (2014) 'The Power of

Philanthropy and Volunteering'. In Huppert, F.A. & Cooper, C.L. *Interventions and Policies to Enhance Well-being: A Complete Reference Guide Vol VI.* London: Wiley & Sons

5 Morelli, S.A. et al (2015) 'Emotional and Instrumental Support Provision Interact To Predict Well-being'. *Emotion*, 15(4), 484–93

6 Ross, W.D. & Brown, L. (2009) *Aristotle: The Nicomachean Ethics.* Oxford: Oxford University Press

7 Curry, O.S. et al (2018) 'Happy To Help? A Systematic Review and Meta-analysis of the Effects of Performing Acts of Kindness on the Well-being of the Actor.' *J. of Experimental Social Psych*, 76, 320–9

8 Hui, B. et al (2020) 'Rewards of Kindness? A Meta-analysis of the Link Between Prosociality and Well-being'. *Psychological Bulletin*, 146(12), 1084–116

9 Ko, K. et al (2021) 'Comparing the Effects of Performing and Recalling Acts of Kindness'. *J. of Positive Psych*, 16(1), 73–81

10 Moll, J. et al (2006) 'Human Fronto-mesolimbic Networks Guide Decisions About Charitable Donation'. *PNAS*, 103(42), 15623–8 See also Lockwood, P.L. et al (2016) 'Neurocomputational Mechanisms of Prosocial Learning and Links to Empathy'. *PNAS*, 113(35), 9763–8

11 Meier, S. & Stutzer, A. (2008) 'Is Volunteering Rewarding in Itself?' *Economica*, 75(297), 39–59

12 Omoto, A.M. et al (2000) 'Volunteerism and the Life Course: Investigating Age-Related Agendas for Action'. *Basic and Applied Social Psych*, 22(3), 181–97

13 Kahana E. et al (2013) 'Altruism, Helping, and Volunteering: Pathways To Well-being in Late Life'. *J. of Aging Health*. 25(1), 159–87

14 Okun M.A. et al (2013) 'Volunteering by Older Adults and Risk of Mortality: A Meta-analysis'. *Psych and Aging*, 28(2), 564–77

15 Guo, Q. et al (2018) 'Beneficial Effects of Pro-social Behaviour

on Physical Well-being in Chinese Samples'. *Asian J. of Social Psychology*, 21(1–2), 22–31

16 Trew, J.L. & Alden, L.E. (2015) 'Kindness Reduces Avoidance Goals in Socially Anxious Individuals'. *Motivation & Emotion*, 39, 892–907

17 Konrath (2014) 'The Power of Philanthropy', 392

18 Lyubomirsky, S. et al (2005) 'Pursuing Happiness: The Architecture of Sustainable Change'. *Review of General Psych*, 9, 111–31

19 Lyubomirsky, S. & Layous, K. (2013) 'How Do Simple Positive Activities Increase Well-being?' *Current Directions in Psychological Science*, 22(1), 57–62

20 Harris, M.B. (1977) 'Effects of Altruism on Mood'. *J. of Social Psych,* 102(2), 197–208

21 Hui (2020) 'Rewards of Kindness?'

22 Li, Y. & Ferraro, K. F. (2005) 'Volunteering and Depression in Later Life: Social Benefit or Selection Processes?' *Journal of Health and Social Behavior*, 46, 68–84

23 Rowland, L. & Curry, O.S. (2019) 'A Range of Kindness Activities Boost Happiness'. *J. of Social Psych* 159(3), 340–3

24 Aknin, L.B. et al (2013) 'Does Social Connection Turn Good Deeds into Good Feelings? On the Value of Putting the 'Social' in Prosocial Spending'. *International Journal of Happiness and Development* 1(2), 155–71

25 Aknin, Does Social Connection, 2013, 155–71

3 Don't get too hung up on motives

1 Abie meets his kidney donor, Good Morning America, 29 July 2019: https://www.goodmorningamerica.com/wellness/video/man-meets-kidney-donor-saved-life-live-gma-64628296

2 You can hear more from Abie in *The Anatomy of Kindness*, a series I presented on BBC Radio 4 produced by Geraldine Fitzgerald and Erika Wright, 16 March 2022: https://www.bbc.co.uk/sounds/play/moo15bdb.

3 This paper has an excellent summary of the different types of altruistic motivation: Curry, O.S. et al (2018) 'Happy To Help? A Systematic Review and Meta-analysis of the Effects of Performing Acts of Kindness on the Well-being of the Actor.' *J. of Experimental Social Psych*, 76, 320–9

4 Gyatso, T., The Fourteenth Dalai Lama. 'Compassion and the Individual': https://www.dalailama.com/messages/compassion-and-human-values/compassion.

5 For a nice description of these different kinds of altruism see Curry, Happy to help?, 2018

6 You can hear more of Lyndall Stein talking to me in *The Anatomy of Kindness* on BBC Radio 4, 16 March 2022: https://www.bbc.co.uk/sounds/play/moo15bdb.

7 Raihani, N.J. & Smith, S. (2015) 'Competitive Helping in Online Giving'. *Current Biology,* 25(9), 1183–6

8 Marsh, A.A. et al (2014) 'Neural and Cognitive Characteristics of Extraordinary Altruists'. *PNAS*, 111, 15036–411

9 Vieira, J.B. et al (2015) 'Psychopathic Traits Are Associated With Cortical and Subcortical Volume Alterations in Healthy Individuals'. *Social Cognitive & Affective Neuroscience* 10(12), 1693–704

10 Abigail Marsh in part two of *The Anatomy of Kindness*, BBC Radio 4, 16 March 2022: https://www.bbc.co.uk/sounds/play/moo15bdb.

11 Fisher, J.D. et al (1982) 'Recipient Reactions to Aid'. *Psychological Bulletin*, 91(1), 27–54

12 Konrath, S. et al (2016) 'The Strategic Helper: Narcissism and Prosocial Motives and Behaviors'. *Current Psych*, 35, 182–94

13 The story of Pete features in this video posted on the BBC Essex Twitter: https://twitter.com/BBCEssex/status/1399977511191261185?s=20.

14 There's a good description of this in Aknin, L.B. et al (2013) 'Making a Difference Matters: Impact Unlocks the Emotional Benefits of Prosocial Spending'. *J. of Economic Behavior & Organization,* 88, 90–5

15 Mathur, VA. et al (2010) 'Neural Basis of Extraordinary Empathy and Altruistic Motivation'. *NeuroImage,* 51(4), 1468–75

16 Bolton, M. (2019) *How to Resist: Turn Protest to Power.* London: Bloomsbury

3½ Social media is full of kindness (OK, not full, but it is there)

1 Brady, W.J. et al (2021) 'How Social Learning Amplifies Moral Outrage Expression in Online Social Networks'. *Science Advances,* 7(33)

2 You can play the game yourself at: https://www.getbadnews. com/#intro. Sander van der Linden has also developed a new game about Covid misinformation: www.goviralgame.com/ books/go-viral/play.

3 Basol, M. et al (2020) 'Good News about Bad News: Gamified Inoculation Boosts Confidence and Cognitive Immunity Against Fake News'. *J. of Cognition,* 3(1), 2

4 Cat vibing to street drummer remix, 4 December 2020: https:// www.youtube.com/watch?v=sq6NcdjLWB8.

5 Buchanan, K. et al (2021) 'Brief Exposure to Social Media During the COVID-19 Pandemic: Doom-scrolling Has Negative Emotional Consequences, but Kindness-scrolling Does Not'. *PLoS One,* 16(10)

4 Kind people can be winners

1   Hall & Partners (2019) Employee Research

2   Diener, E. & Seligman, M.E.P. (2002) 'Very Happy People'. *Psychological Science*, 13(1), 81–4

3   Walumbwa, F.O. & Schaubroeck, J. (2009) 'Leader Personality Traits and Employee Voice Behavior: Mediating Roles of Ethical Leadership and Work Group Psychological Safety'. *J. of Applied Psych*, 94(5), 1275–86

4   Zenger, J. & Folkman, J. 'I'm the Boss! Why Should I Care If You Like Me?', *Harvard Business Review*, 2 May 2013: https://hbr.org/2013/05/im-the-boss-why-should-i-care.

5   Walumbwa, F.O. et al (2011) 'Linking Ethical Leadership to Employee Performance: The Roles of Leader–Member Exchange, Self-efficacy, and Organizational Identification'. *Organizational Behavior and Human Decision Processes*, 115(2), 204–13

6   Brown, M.E. & Treviño, L.K. (2006) 'Ethical Leadership: A Review and Future Directions'. *The Leadership Quarterly*, 17, 595–616

7   Vianello, M. et al (2010) 'Elevation at Work: The Effects of Leaders' Moral Excellence'. *J. of Positive Psych*, 5(5), 390–411

8   'Spain Triathlete Gives Up Medal to Rival Who Went Wrong Way', BBC News, 20 September 2020: https://www.bbc.co.uk/news/world-54224410.

9   Brand, G. 'Why England Needed Gareth Southgate: How Off-field Influence Helped Build Culture of Success', 11 July 2021: https://www.skysports.com/football/news/12016/12351872/why-england-needed-gareth-southgate-how-off-field-influence-helped-build-culture-of-success.

10 Podsakoff, N.P. et al (2009) 'Individual- And Organizational-level

Consequences of Organizational Citizenship Behaviors: A Meta-analysis'. *J. of Applied Psych*, 94(1), 122–41

11 'Donald Trump Calls for More Civility as He Attacks Media and Democrats at Charlotte Rally' USA Today, 26 October 2018: https://eu.usatoday.com/story/news/politics/2018/10/26/donald-trump-calls-more-civility-attacks-media-and-democrats-charlotte-rally/1778539002/

12 Frimer, J.A. & Skitka, L.J. (2018) 'The Montagu Principle: Incivility Decreases Politicians' Public Approval, Even With Their Political Base'. *J. of Personality and Social Psych*, 115(5), 845–86

13 Roets, A. & Van Hiel, A. (2009) 'The Ideal Politician: Impact of Voters' Ideology'. *Personality and Individual Differences*, 46(1), 60–5

5 Kindness comes from seeing other people's points of view

1 Hazlitt, W. (1900) 'On The Conduct of Life'. In Carr, F. (Ed.) *Essays of William Hazlitt*. London: Walter Scott. 199

2 See also Lamm, C. et al (2011) 'Meta-analytic Evidence for Common and Distinct Neural Networks Associated With Directly Experienced Pain and Empathy for Pain'. *NeuroImage*, 54(3), 2492–502

3 There's an excellent summary of this work in Singer, T. & Klimecki, O.M. (2014) Empathy and Compassion. *Current Biology*, 24(18), 875–8

4 Allen, A.P. et al (2016) 'The Trier Social Stress Test: Principles and Practice'. *Neurobiology of Stress*, 6, 113–26

5 Birkett M.A. (2011) 'The Trier Social Stress Test Protocol for Inducing Psychological Stress'. *J. of Visualized Experiments*, 56, 3238

6 Fonagy, P. 'Kindness Can Work Wonders. Especially for the Vulnerable', Guardian, 17 May 2020: https://www.theguardian.

com/society/2020/may/17/kindness-can-work-wonders-especially-for-the-vulnerable.

7   Catapano, R. et al (2019) 'Perspective Taking and Self-Persuasion: Why "Putting Yourself in Their Shoes" Reduces Openness to Attitude Change'. *Psychological Science*, 30(3), 424–35

8   Gilbert, P. (2009) *The Compassionate Mind*. London: Constable

9   To try these exercises I do recommend Gilbert (2009), *The Compassionate Mind*; the exercises are described in detail on page 295.

10 Schumann, K. et al (2014) 'Addressing the Empathy Deficit: Beliefs About the Malleability of Empathy Predict Effortful Responses When Empathy Is Challenging'. *J. of Personality & Social Psych*, 107(3), 475–93

11 Batson, C.D. et al (1997) 'Perspective Taking: Imagining How Another Feels Versus Imagining How You Would Feel'. *Personality & Social Psych Bulletin*, 23(7), 751–8

12 Batson, C.D. et al (2004) 'Benefits and Liabilities of Empathy-induced Altruism'. In Miller, A.G. (Ed.) *The Social Psychology of Good and Evil*. New York: The Guilford Press

13 Batson, C.D. & Ahmad, N. (2001) 'Empathy-induced Altruism in a Prisoner's Dilemma II: What if the Target of Empathy Has Defected?' *European J. of Social Psych*, 31(1), 25–36

14 Blythe, J. et al (2021) 'Fostering Ocean Empathy Through Future Scenarios'. *People & Nature*, 3(6) 1284–96. You can watch the pessimistic scenario here: https://www.youtube.com/watch?v=-dYiaErO1aM.

15 For a brilliant summary of research on inducing empathy see Konrath, S. & Grynberg, D. (2016) 'The Positive (And Negative) Psychology of Empathy'. In Watt, D.F. & Panksepp, J. (Eds.) *Psychology and Neurobiology of Empathy*. New York: Nova Biomedical Books

16 Batson, C.D. et al (2002) 'Empathy, Attitudes, and Action: Can Feeling for a Member of a Stigmatized Group Motivate One to Help the Group?' *Personality & Social Psych Bulletin*, 28(12), 1656–66

17 Singer & Klimecki (2014) 'Empathy and Compassion'

18 Klimecki, O.M. et al (2014) 'Differential Pattern of Functional Brain Plasticity After Compassion and Empathy Training'. *Social Cognitive and Affective Neuroscience*, 9(6), 873–9

19 Bloom, P. (2017) *Against Empathy*. London: Bodley Head

20 Tajfel, H. et al (1971) 'Social Categorization and Intergroup Behaviour'. *European J. of Social Psychology*, 1, 149–78

21 Pelham, B.W. et al (2002) 'Why Susie Sells Seashells by the Seashore: Implicit Egotism and Major Life Decisions'. *J. of Personality & Social Psych*, 82(4), 469–87

22 Hodson, G. & Olson, J.M. (2005) 'Testing the Generality of the Name Letter Effect: Name Initials and Everyday Attitudes'. *Personality & Social Psych Bulletin*, 31(8), 1099–111

23 Decety, J. et al (2010) 'Physicians Down-regulate Their Pain Empathy Response: An Event-related Brain Potential Study'. *NeuroImage*, 50(4), 1676–82

24 Michelbrink, L.E. (2015) Masters Thesis. 'Is Empathy Always a Good Thing? The Ability To Regulate Cognitive and Affective Empathy in a Medical Setting'. Leiden University Institute of Psychology

25 You can hear me interviewing Brett Campbell in *The Evidence* on BBC World Service, 31 October 2021: https://www.bbc.co.uk/programmes/w3ct2zpk.

26 Aron, A. et al (1997) 'The Experimental Generation of Interpersonal Closeness: A Procedure and Some Preliminary Findings'. *Personality & Social Psych Bulletin*, 23, 363–77

27 Sprecher, S. (2021) 'Closeness and Other Affiliative Outcomes

Generated From the Fast Friends Procedure: A Comparison With a Small-talk Task and Unstructured Self-disclosure and the Moderating Role of Mode of Communication'. *J. of Social & Personal Relationships*, 38(5), 1452–71

28 Page-Gould, E. et al (2008) 'With a Little Help From My Cross-group Friend: Reducing Anxiety in Intergroup Contexts Through Cross-group Friendship'. *J. of Personality & Social Psych*, 95(5), 1080–94

29 Kardas, M. et al (2021) 'Overly Shallow?: Miscalibrated Expectations Create a Barrier To Deeper Conversation'. *J. of Personality & Social Psych*, 122(3), 367–98

30 Sandstrom, G.M. & Boothby, E.J. (2021) 'Why Do People Avoid Talking to Strangers? A Mini Meta-analysis of Predicted Fears and Actual Experiences Talking to a Stranger'. *Self and Identity*, 20(1), 47–71

31 Sandstrom (2021) 'Why Do People Avoid'

32 Mannix, K. (2021) *Listen: How to Find the Words for Tender Conversations*. London: William Collins

33 Shafak, E. (2020) *How to Stay Sane in an Age of Division*. London: Wellcome Collection

34 Tamir, D.I. et al (2016) 'Reading Fiction and Reading Minds: The Role of Simulation in the Default Network'. *Social Cognitive & Affective Neuroscience*, 11(2), 215–24

35 Oatley, K. (2016) 'Fiction: Simulation of Social Worlds'. *Trends in Cognitive Science* 20(8), 618–28

36 Mar, R.A. et al (2006) 'Bookworms Versus Nerds: Exposure to Fiction Versus Non-fiction, Divergent Associations With Social Ability, and the Simulation of Fictional Social Worlds'. *J. of Research in Personality*, 40(5), 694–712

37 Mar, Bookworms Versus Nerds 2006, 694–712

38 Oatley (2016) 'Fiction'

39 Johnson, D.R. (2012) 'Transportation Into a Story Increases Empathy, Prosocial Behavior, and Perceptual Bias Toward Fearful Expressions'. *Personality & Individual Differences*, 52(2), 150–5

40 Bal, P.M. & Veltkamp, M. (2013) 'How Does Fiction Reading Influence Empathy? An Experimental Investigation on the Role of Emotional Transportation'. *PLos One* 8(1)

41 Shapiro, J. & Rucker, L. (2003) 'Can Poetry Make Better Doctors? Teaching the Humanities and Arts to Medical Students and Residents at the University of California, Irvine, College of Medicine'. *Academic Medicine*, 78(10), 953–7

6 Anyone can be a hero

1 The Comprehensive Guide to the Victoria and George Cross, http://www.vconline.org.uk/johnson-g-beharry-vc/4585968848.html.

2 'Soldier Wins VC for Iraq Bravery', BBC News, 18 March 2005: http://news.bbc.co.uk/1/hi/uk/4358921.stm.

3 Matthew Croucher was widely quoted discussing his bravery, including at telegraph.co.uk/news/uknews/2445513/Royal-Marine-who-jumped-on-grenade-awarded-George-Cross.html.

4 Price, J. (2015) *Heroes of Postman's Park*. Stroud: The History Press, 37

5 Price (2015) *Heroes*, 42

6 Price (2015) *Heroes*, 43

7 Price (2015) *Heroes*, 88

8 Price (2015) *Heroes*, 135

9 Price (2015) *Heroes*, 136

10 Haney, C. et al (1973) 'A Study of Prisoners and Guards in a Simulated Prison'. *Naval Research Review*, 30

11 Haslam, S.A. et al (2019) 'Rethinking the Nature of Cruelty: The Role of Identity Leadership in the Stanford Prison Experiment'. *American Psychologist*, 74(7), 809–22

12 Sword, R.K.M. & Zimbardo, P. 'We Need to Embrace Heroic Imagination', *Psychology Today*, 30 March 2021: https://www.psychologytoday.com/ie/blog/the-time-cure/202103/we-need-embrace-heroic-imagination.

13 Franco, Z.E. et al (2018) 'Heroism Research: A Review of Theories, Methods, Challenges, and Trends'. *J. of Humanistic Psychology*, 58(4), 382–96. For the roots of Zimbardo's work on heroism see also Zimbardo, P. (2007) *The Lucifer Effect: How Good People Turn Evil*. London: Rider Books

14 Kinsella, E.L. et al (2015) 'Zeroing in on Heroes: A Prototype Analysis of Hero Features'. *J. of Personality & Social Psych*, 108(1), 114–27

15 Hock, R.R. (2002) *Forty Studies That Changed Psychology*. New Jersey: Prentice Hall. 294

16 Franco, Z.E. et al (2011) 'Heroism: A Conceptual Analysis and Differentiation between Heroic Action and Altruism'. *Review of General Psych*, 15(2), 99–113

17 Gallagher, J. 'Oxford Vaccine: How Did They Make It So Quickly?', BBC News, 23 November 2020: https://www.bbc.co.uk/news/health-55041371.

18 Smith, S.F. et al (2013) 'Are Psychopaths and Heroes Twigs off the Same Branch? Evidence From College, Community, and Presidential Samples'. *J. of Research in Personality*, 47(5), 634–46

19 Levine, M. et al (2005) 'Identity and Emergency Intervention: How Social Group Membership and Inclusiveness of Group Boundaries Shape Helping Behavior'. *Personality & Social Psych Bulletin*, 31(4), 443–53

20 Drury, J. et al (2009) 'The Nature of Collective Resilience: Survivor

Reactions to the 2005 London Bombings'. *International Journal of Mass Emergencies and Disasters*, 27, 66–95

21 Gornall, S. 'Skiing by Braille', *Ski Magazine*, 16 September 2009: https://www.skimag.com/adventure/skiing-by-braille-0/

22 Liebst, L.S. et al (2021) 'Cross-national CCTV Footage Shows Low Victimization Risk for Bystander Interveners in Public Conflicts'. *Psych of Violence, 11*(1), 11–18

23 Takooshian, H. (1983) 'Getting Involved – The Safe Way'. *Social Action and the Law,* 9(2)

24 Takooshian, H. & Barsumyan, S.E. (1992) 'Bystander Behaviour, Street Crime and the Law'. In Levin, B.I. (Ed.) *Studies in Deviance*. Moscow: Institute for Sociology

7 Remember to be kind to yourself

1 Gilbert, P. (2011) 'Fears of Compassion: Development of Three Self-report Measures'. *Psych and Psychotherapy: theory, research and practice*, 84, 239–55

2 Longe, O. et al (2010) 'Having a Word With Yourself: Neural Correlates of Self-criticism and Self-reassurance'. *NeuroImage*, 49, 1849–56

3 Kirby, J.N. et al (2019) 'The "Flow" of Compassion: A Meta-analysis of the Fears of Compassion Scales and Psychological Functioning'. *Clinical Psych Review*, 70, 26–39

4 Gilbert (2011) 'Fears of Compassion'

5 Gilbert (2011) 'Fears of Compassion'

6 MacBeth, A. & Gumley, A. (2012) 'Exploring Compassion: A Meta-analysis of the Association Between Self-compassion and Psychopathology'. *Clinical Psych Review*, 32(6), 545–52

7 Various studies cited in Neff, K.D. & Germer, C.K. (2013) 'A

Pilot Study and Randomized Controlled Trail of the Mindful Self-compassion Program'. *J. of Clinical Psych*, 69(1), 28–44

8   López, A. et al (2018) 'Compassion for Others and Self-Compassion: Levels, Correlates, and Relationship With Psychological Well-being'. *Mindfulness,* 9(1), 325–31

9   Matos, M. et al (2021) 'Fears of Compassion Magnify the Harmful Effects of Threat of COVID-19 on Mental Health and Social Safeness Across 21 Countries'. *Clinical Psych & Psychotherapy*, 28(6), 1317–33

10 Matos, M. et al (2022) 'Compassion Protects Mental Health and Social Safeness During the COVID-19 Pandemic Across 21 Countries'. *Mindfulness*, 1–18. Advance online publication.

11 Neff, K.D. (2003) 'The Development and Validation of a Scale to Measure Self-Compassion'. *Self and Identity*, 2, 223–50

12 Marshall, S.L. et al (2020) 'Is Self-Compassion Selfish? The Development of Self-Compassion, Empathy, and Prosocial Behavior in Adolescence'. *J. of Research on Adolescence*, 30 Suppl 2, 472–84

13 See Marshall (2020) 'Is Self-Compassion Selfish?' for a lovely summary of all of these studies.

14 Neff (2003) 'Development and Validation'

15 Leary, M.R. et al (2007) 'Self-Compassion and Reactions To Unpleasant Self-relevant Events: The Implications of Treating Oneself Kindly'. *J. of Personality and Social Psych*, 92(5), 887–904

16 Wohl, M.J.A et al (2010) 'I Forgive Myself, Now I Can Study: How Self-Forgiveness for Procrastinating Can Reduce Future Procrastination'. *Personality and Individual Differences*, 48(7), 803–8

17 Nelson, S.K. et al (2016) 'Do Unto Others or Treat Yourself? The Effects of Prosocial and Self-Focused Behavior on Psychological Flourishing'. *Emotion*, 16(6), 850–61

18 You can see a film I made about virtual reality avatars for the

BBC here, 19 November 2014: https://www.bbc.co.uk/news/av/health-30117385.

19 Falconer, C. et al (2016) 'Embodying Self-Compassion Within Virtual Reality and Its Effects on Patients With Depression'. *British J. of Psychiatry Open*, 2(1), 74–80

20 Leary et al (2008) 'Self-compassion'

21 Neff, K.D. & Germer, C.K. (2013) 'A Pilot Study and Randomized Controlled Trail of the Mindful Self-Compassion Program'. *J. of Clinical Psych*, 69(1), 28–44

22 Germer, C. (2009) *The Mindful Path to Self-Compassion*. New York: Guilford Press

A prescription for kindness

1 Otake, K. et al (2006) 'Happy People Become Happier Through Kindness: A Counting Kindnesses Intervention'. *Journal of Happiness Studies*, 7, 361–75

2 Sturm, V.E. et al (2020) 'Big Smile, Small Self: Awe Walks Promote Prosocial Positive Emotions in Older Adults'. *Emotion*. Advance online publication

INDEX

CLAUDIA HAMMOND is an award-winning writer and broadcaster. She is Visiting Professor of the Public Understanding of Psychology at the University of Sussex and is the presenter of BBC Radio 4's *All in the Mind*. She has been awarded the President's Medal from the British Academy, the British Psychological Society's Public Engagement & Media Award, Mind's Making a Difference Award and the British Neuroscience Association's Public Understanding of Neuroscience Award. She is the author of *Emotional Rollercoaster*, *Mind Over Money*, *Time Warped*, which won the Aeon Transmission Award and the BPS' Best Popular Science Book Award, and *The Art of Rest*, which was also shortlisted for the latter and was picked for Waterstones Non-Fiction Book of the Month.

@claudiahammond | claudiahammond.com